ABIDING HOPE

Abiding Hope

Encouragement in the Shadow of Death

ANN HAGMANN

UPPER ROOM BOOKS®
NASHVILLE

The Upper Room® Web site: http://www.upperroom.org

UPPER ROOM®, UPPER ROOM BOOKS®, and design logos are trademarks owned by The Upper Room®, Nashville, Tennessee. All rights reserved.

Scripture quotations are from the New Revised Standard Version of the Bible, copyright 1989, Division of Christian Education of the National Council of the Churches of Christ in the United States of America. Used by permission. All rights reserved.

Names of persons, except for Jin Young, Terri, and Donna, have been changed to protect their privacy.

Excerpt from "Desiderata." Copyright © 1927 by Max Ehrmann. All rights reserved. Reprinted by permission of Robert L. Bell, Melrose, MA 02176.

Cover and interior design: Ed Maksimowicz
Cover illustration: David David Gallery, Philadelphia/SuperStock
Author photo: Janet Lynn Photography
First printing: 2002

Library of Congress Cataloging-in-Publication Data

Hagmann, Ann, 1948–
    Abiding hope : encouragement in the shadow of death / Ann Hagmann.
        p. cm.
    Includes bibliographical references.
    ISBN 0-8358-0959-5
    1. Death—Religious aspects—Christianity. I. Title.
BT825.H25 2002
242'.4—dc21

                                      2001045444

Printed in the United States of America

In loving gratitude to my patients
and their families and friends,
who shared their vulnerability
and allowed me the sacred trust
of journeying with them
during a time of transition.

And in loving admiration for
the women and men of Hospice Austin,
with whom I have the great privilege of serving.

CONTENTS

PART THREE: THE SHEPHERD'S TABLE FEEDS US

PART FOUR: THE SHEPHERD'S ANOINTING SUSTAINS US

ACKNOWLEDGMENTS

I am grateful to Nancy Ackley, who planted the first seed for this book when she asked me if I was writing about my hospice experience. I am also grateful to Mary Brewington and Suzanne Franka for their work of reviewing my text and making excellent suggestions for change. Special thanks to Upper Room Books Executive Editor JoAnn Miller, who opened a door for this book and allowed it to be birthed in me.

I would also like to express appreciation to Jin Young, Terri, and Donna for allowing parts of their stories to appear in this book.

INTRODUCTION

Amazing things happen when we pray earnestly. Recently while I was walking and praying the Twenty-third Psalm, a revelation hit me: As a hospice chaplain I walk daily in the valley of the shadow of death. This is where I live.

Hospices provide end-of-life care for terminally ill people and their families and friends. This care is usually provided in the patient's own home, though it can also be given in hospitals, nursing and personal care homes, and hospice inpatient facilities. My vocation as a chaplain with Hospice Austin includes normal and on-call emergency work in each of these settings. Hospice Austin is a large, nonprofit hospice that covers five counties in central Texas. We have a daily load of 180 to 220 patients.

I passionately love my work, but when you dwell in the shadow of death, you must focus on positives. The key word here is *focus*—the ability to apply your attention to one place so that you have the strength to endure the tasks of life you are given. I wrote this book for ill persons and their caregivers and loved ones. I hope that the book will also be a valuable resource for workers in the hospice and medical fields.

Whether your illness or caregiving situation lasts for a short time or for twenty years, you need nurturing and sustaining in the face of illness and its significant changes. Many times in the process of illness or dying, the person you have known and loved ceases to be, and a new person takes his or her place in a changing body. This is a significant change, both for the ill one and the caregivers. Everyone involved needs spiritual and emotional support for the journey. I hope this book leads you on a path toward that provision.

In the case of ill persons who cannot read this book for themselves, caregivers can read and share it with them. The devotions may open the door to helpful conversations. If the ill person is incapacitated beyond involvement, I especially hope that the book nurtures you, the caregivers and/or loved ones.

Each devotion includes a key verse or two from a psalm, an introductory situation or question, and then the psalm for the day (which is often an excerpt rather than the entire psalm). After my reflections, I offer a prayer suggestion and a prayer. When you pray, feel free to substitute the words that best describe your situation.

The book has four sections that use the imagery of the Twenty-third Psalm: the shepherd's rod, staff, table, and anointing. Each section contains ten psalms that I selected for their sustaining power.

> Even though I walk through the darkest valley,[1]
>   I fear no evil;
> for you are with me;
>   your *rod* and your *staff*—
>   they comfort me.
>
> You prepare a *table* before me
>   in the presence of my enemies;
> you *anoint* my head with oil;
>   my cup overflows.
> Surely goodness and mercy
>   shall follow me all the days of my life,
> and I shall dwell in the house of the LORD
>   my whole life long.
>
> Psalm 23:4-6, italics mine

The rod represents God's defense of us; the staff, God's redirection of our feet; the table, God's provision for us in the face of our enemies; the anointing, God's abundant grace and mercy that is present in the midst of hardship and change.

May these psalms, reflections, and prayers help you experience genuine encounter with yourself and with the One who gives you life. May they also encourage a strong and empowering faith.

Even though I walk through
the valley of the shadow of death,
I fear no evil;
for you are with me;
your . . . rod . . . comfort[s] me.

Psalm 23:4

PART ONE | # The Shepherd's Rod Defends Us

FEAR NO EVIL

Even though I walk through the valley of the shadow of death,
I fear no evil;
for you are with me;
your rod and your staff—
they comfort me.

Psalm 23:4

When I arrived at Michael's home, his whole family had gathered. His wife was in deep shock, and his five children and their spouses were all busy trying to help solve a situation that was out of their control. Michael's lung condition had suddenly progressed to the point that he could not breathe on his own. I sat on his footstool for more than an hour while he took five or six breathing treatments. Eventually he breathed comfortably with an oxygen mask, and his heart slowed down. He would be all right for now.

During this time Michael and I talked about golfing, his family, and his business. Later one of his sons thanked me for knowing the right words to say to calm his father's fears. Truth is, I had no idea what I would say before I arrived or before the conversation unfolded. I simply and prayerfully went where I sensed the Holy Spirit leading. The conversation was about everyday stuff, and it touched on Michael's spiritual condition. I was blessed to be a messenger who helped bring peace.

What helps calm your fears?

PSALM 23

The LORD is my shepherd, I shall not want.
He makes me lie down in green pastures;
    he leads me beside still waters;

he restores my soul.
He leads me in right paths for his name's sake.

Even though I walk through the valley of the shadow of
    death,
    I fear no evil; for you are with me;
    your rod and your staff—
        they comfort me.

You prepare a table before me in the presence of my
    enemies;
you anoint my head with oil;
    my cup overflows.
Surely goodness and mercy shall follow me
    all the days of my life,
and I shall dwell in the house of the LORD my whole
    life long.

Michael shared with me his amazement at the peace he felt. Though not a religious man, he believed in God and that somehow by God's grace he could live through this moment and this illness.

The Twenty-third Psalm is a beautiful expression of perfect trust—trust that God is with us and will meet our needs. This psalm is the one most commonly used at funerals, yet it is an equally powerful psalm for living, for trusting, and for entrusting ourselves to God and God's care of us. God's provision will be enough, more than enough, for our cup overflows.

Oddly enough, while we may hesitate to trust in the Creator's love for us, we trust utter strangers with our lives each day. Think about that. For example, when I open my box of Raisin Bran, I expect to find two full scoops of raisins. I trust that the cereal is safe to eat. I trust that the producer, manufacturer, and deliverer have been honest with me. We cannot live without trusting others. The Twenty-third Psalm invites us to trust in the One who gave us life and who journeys with us through our lives.

Fear is a very real emotion. It can even be helpful and save our lives, but fear that overwhelms us and produces great anxiety is not healthy. We need a weapon to fight against it. Our faith is the best weapon. I encourage you, in the way that feels most appropriate, to step out and actively trust that God will calm your fears and provide for your needs.

PRAYER SUGGESTION

Sit quietly for a few minutes, then reread the Twenty-third Psalm. Savor each word. Visualize the shepherd providing for his sheep. Read the psalm once more and visualize the One who loves you taking care of you.

PRAYER

*Shepherd of our souls, we trust your rod to defend us from
    the evils that befall us.
Free us from fear that is destructive.
Deliver us from all our enemies.
Lead us into safe places, so that even though we walk
    through the valley of the shadow of death, we will fear
    no evil but will trust in your goodness toward us.
Help us to turn toward you, O Lord our God, and find
    peace. Restore our souls. Amen.*

ASKING FOR HELP

Incline your ear to me; rescue me speedily.
Be a rock of refuge for me, a strong fortress to save me.
Psalm 31:2

Ironic as it is, we are always shocked when we realize that we have little control over our lives or the lives of those around us. We thought we were in charge. After all, aren't we independent and self-sufficient? But serious illness throws a wrench into our illusion of control.

What should we do when we are in the midst of circumstances beyond our control? It is wise to realize that we are helpless, to assess our support and resources, and to act to seek the help we need. Reinhold Niebuhr's Serenity Prayer provides guidance here:

> God, grant me the serenity to accept the things I cannot change,
> the courage to change the things I can,
> and the wisdom to know the difference.

Certainly, illness is a wake-up call to rely on God. The wonderful thing is that even though the situation prodding us to rely on One greater than ourselves is terrible, it also bears the wonderful fruit of faith. All we need to do is ask God for help and then be alert to God's provision.

PSALM 31:1-5, 9-10, 14-16, 24

In you, O LORD, I seek refuge;
    do not let me ever be put to shame;
    in your righteousness deliver me.
Incline your ear to me;

rescue me speedily.
Be a rock of refuge for me,
    a strong fortress to save me.

You are indeed my rock and my fortress;
    for your name's sake lead me and guide me,
take me out of the net that is hidden for me,
    for you are my refuge.
Into your hand I commit my spirit;
    you have redeemed me, O LORD, faithful God.

. . . .

Be gracious to me, O LORD, for I am in distress;
    my eye wastes away from grief, my soul and body also.
For my life is spent with sorrow, and my years with sighing;
    my strength fails because of my misery,
    and my bones waste away.

. . . .

But I trust in you, O LORD; I say, "You are my God."
My times are in your hand;
    deliver me from the hand of my enemies and persecutors.
Let your face shine upon your servant; save me in your
    steadfast love.

. . . .

Be strong, and let your heart take courage,
    all you who wait for the LORD.

Generally, people change out of aspiration or desperation. We can aspire to grow in our faith and seek avenues to achieve that growth, such as becoming involved in a study or devoting time to a community service project. We can also grasp and cling to faith out of desperation; we cry out to God to rescue us because our lives are out of control. Fortunately, both paths lead to God and God's love for us.

Psalm 31 is a passionate cry to the all-powerful God. Circumstances are out of control, and the psalmist is grieved. His soul and body waste away. His life is spent with sorrow; his strength fails him. He is acquainted with dis-ease of body, soul, and spirit. He knows our plight. Yet out of this depth of affliction, the psalmist rises to shout, "But I trust in you, O LORD; I say, 'You are my God.' / My times are in your hand." The psalmist has faith in God's character and in God's steadfast love.

The key is to commit our spirit into God's hands. Sometimes we do not have enough experience with God to produce the faith we need to trust God. At such times acting *as if* we have that faith is appropriate. If we imagine life as traveling on a sea, then to trust in God's sustaining and redeeming power is to float on that sea, trusting in where God leads us. It is not to swim or to tread water, nor to act on our own without consulting God. The psalmist cries, "Incline your ear," "rescue me speedily," "be a rock of refuge, . . . a strong fortress to save me."

Feeling despair is natural when we are forced to come to terms with an unwanted illness that affects our loved one or us. When we break through the denial, we can feel overwhelmed at the possible path ahead of us. How will we possibly make it? Despair is real in our hearts and lives. But the psalmist urges us to "be strong, and let your heart take courage / . . . wait for the LORD!" Crying out to God and stepping out in faith will counter our despair and help save us from its deadly grasp.

I met Kyle during a weekend crisis when his pain became unmanageable. Kyle was stricken in body, soul, and spirit. His disease had progressed to the point that he could not stay alone. He couldn't afford round-the-clock nursing care. His two grown children lived nearby, but their demands and responsibilities precluded either of them being able to care for him for any significant amount of time. Besides, Kyle couldn't bear the thought of his children bathing him and taking care of his basic hygiene.

Kyle cried out to God; he wailed and moaned. After we talked, he decided to call the church from which he had been disconnected since his children had grown up. Fortunately for him, the minister who visited him had pursued interests in spiritual formation. She taught Kyle about simple discernment prayer, suggesting that he ask God simple yes/no questions, then listen for God's answer by "trying on" different answers and paying attention to his emotions of peace or distress. If he felt peaceful after trying on an answer, she said, then that most likely was the direction in which God was leading. But if he felt distressed, then the answer was probably not God's direction.

Kyle began floating on God's sea, and through prayerful discernment a plan emerged. He was placed on the residency list for our inpatient facility. It took him eight days to get in, but during that waiting period his children were able to take off work and stay with him. With the help of home health aides, his physical needs were met without too much loss of dignity. Kyle was able to work through his despair by prayer—prayer expressed as words and as active trusting. God responded to Kyle's cry just as the Loving One will respond to our cries.

PRAYER SUGGESTION

When despair, fear, anxiety, or worry strike, lift a quick prayer to God. Your prayer can be as brief as "Lord, help me" or "Holy Spirit, still my heart." (I bought some cards that said "Help, Lord, help!")

Memorize all or part of verse 2: "Incline your ear to me; / rescue me speedily. / Be a rock of refuge for me, / a strong fortress to save me." No matter what happens, hold on to that rock; focus on that fortress.

PRAYER

In you, O God, we seek refuge.
Hide us in your strong fortress; protect us
    from the fear and despair that seek to overwhelm us.
You have brought us this far. Into your hands we commit
    our spirits, our souls, our bodies, and all those we love.

Be gracious to us. We are distressed and brokenhearted.
Our dreams fall around us. You are our God. Our days
  and hours are in your hands.
Deliver us from these enemies.
Help us to be strong.
Let our hearts take courage. Help us to wait for you,
  O Lord our God. Amen.

ETERNAL HOPE

When I look at your heavens,
the work of your fingers,
the moon and the stars that you have established;
what are human beings that you are mindful of them,
mortals that you care for them?

Psalm 8:3-4

We all need hope. Hebrews 11:1 says, "Now faith is the assurance of things hoped for, the conviction of things not seen." Hope is essential to faith. Hope anticipates that things will go as we need or want them to. It believes God is in the midst of our situations, working to bring good. A terminally ill person may hope not to have much pain as the illness progresses. A caregiver may hope for the emotional and spiritual support necessary to carry out his or her tasks.

Hope is an attitude of great importance for spiritual people because it lifts us up. It encourages us. A classic attitude check is to ask yourself this question: If someone gave you an eight-ounce glass with four ounces of water in it, would the glass be half empty or half full? If you answer "half empty," you tend to see what is missing from your life rather than your blessings. If you answer "half full," you probably focus on the blessings, the positives.

I always answered "half full" until I meditated on these words from the Twenty-third Psalm: "Even though I walk through the valley of the shadow of death, / I fear no evil; for you are with me; / . . . you anoint my head with oil; / my cup overflows." I realized that with God's help, my cup is not just half full; it is overflowing!

When we open ourselves to God, our lives overflow with blessings. Whether we seek God's help to love and to care for an ill mate, to forgive an abusive father, or to accept our own bitter pill of illness, God is with us and for us. In all cases, we can confidently hope in God's abundant provision for us, so our cups overflow. God gives us more than enough to cover our need.

PSALM 8:1, 3-9

O Lord, our Sovereign,
    how majestic is your name in all the earth!
You have set your glory above the heavens.

. . . .

When I look at your heavens,
    the work of your fingers,
    the moon and the stars that you have established;
what are human beings that you are mindful of them,
    mortals that you care for them?

Yet you have made them a little lower than God,
    and crowned them with glory and honor.
You have given them dominion over the works of your hands;
    you have put all things under their feet,
    all sheep and oxen, and also the beasts of the field,
    the birds of the air, and the fish of the sea,
    whatever passes along the paths of the seas.

O LORD, our Sovereign,
    how majestic is your name in all the earth!

The great scientist Albert Einstein reportedly said, "There are only two ways to live your life. One is as though nothing is a miracle. The other is as though everything is a miracle." I agree with Einstein; everything is a miracle. The psalmist also supports this view.

I have always been a nature nut, but the reality of the miracle of life was brought home to me in a new way one evening as I left a patient's home to return to mine. Paige, a thoughtful fifty-three-year-old woman, walked me to my car. We looked up together and saw a magnificent full October moon rising. Its incredible amber glow gave us goose bumps. Paige took a deep breath, turned to me, and said, "There is so much more to life than my illness." I responded in a hushed tone, "There is so much more to life than just us." We stood together in the silence for a minute or two; then we hugged and parted, having experienced the touch of the awesomeness of creation.

Similar experiences must have inspired our psalmist to cry out, "When I look at your heavens, / the work of your fingers, / the moon and the stars that you have established; / what are human beings that you are mindful of them, / mortals that you care for them?" If we look at the majesty of the world around us, isn't it incredible to know that the same God who created everything also loves each of us and cares about us as individuals? I am astounded when I realize the interconnectedness of the universe God created. What a wonderful gift God gives to inspire and encourage us! May we let the daily miracles nurture our hope.

PRAYER SUGGESTION

Find a favorite belonging that reflects the wonder of creation and life. Perhaps you only need to look out a window in your home. Or maybe you have photos of a beautiful place, some artwork, seashells, or interesting rocks. When you find yourself feeling down or insignificant, look at your belonging, read Psalm 8, and ponder the miracle of your life and of God's love for you.

I have always been fond of these words from the Desiderata: "You are a child of the universe, no less than the trees and the stars; you have a right to be here." I would add that you have more than a right; you have the gift of life from a caring God. Persevere in fighting discouragement with hope.

PRAYER

*O Lord our God, how majestic is your name in all
   the earth!*
*You fill our cups to overflowing; you bless our lives
   each day.*
Help us to realize the incredible gifts of life you give us.
*Help us to accept our place in this vast and marvelous
   universe.*
*May the beauty and majesty of your creation uplift us and
   remind us of your presence as it calls us to be a people
   of hope. Amen.*

DON'T FEAR SLEEP

I lie down and sleep;
I wake again, for the LORD sustains me.
Psalm 3:5

We can't live without sleep. As I write this devotion, I am taking a course called The Wisdom of Dreams. Our leader, a Jungian psychoanalyst, says that next to air, dreams are our most critical need for survival. He ranks our basic needs in this sequence: air, dreams/sleep, water, food, and shelter.

Dreams are the playground where we process and work through the events of the day. They are a primary means of communication between our unconscious and conscious mind. Scripture shows us that dreams are also avenues for hearing from God.

Whether or not you can recall your dreams, everyone dreams. But without sleep, dreams cannot happen. By measuring the eye movements of sleeping subjects, scientists can interrupt dream periods as soon as they begin. Studies show that people prevented from dreaming begin displaying psychotic behavior within twenty-four to forty-eight hours!

I have always had periods of intense dreaming, especially during times of great stress. For someone under intense stress from caregiving or illness, sleep has even greater significance. Do you ever have trouble sleeping? Consider what the psalmist says about sleep.

PSALM 3

O LORD, how many are my foes!
Many are rising against me;
    many are saying to me, "There is no help for you in God."

But you, O LORD, are a shield around me,
>   my glory, and the one who lifts up my head.
I cry aloud to the LORD, and he answers me from his holy hill.

I lie down and sleep;
>   I wake again, for the LORD sustains me.
I am not afraid of ten thousands of people
>   who have set themselves against me all around.

Rise up, O LORD! Deliver me, O my God!
For you strike all my enemies on the cheek;
>   you break the teeth of the wicked.

Deliverance belongs to the LORD;
>   may your blessing be on your people!

Wilson and his wife are a good example of how underlying fears can grip us and affect our sleep. Wilson developed brain cancer. For a time in our journey through the valley of the shadow of death, Wilson's wife thought his greatest fear was going to bed at night. She believed he was frightened that he might not regain consciousness, that he might slip into a coma or die during his sleep. But in our conversations Wilson revealed that the most fearful time for him was waking each morning and not knowing what condition his body would be in. Would he be able to talk clearly today? Would he be able to use his hands?

Life has an enemy who first pops up in the third chapter of Genesis, questioning God's trustworthiness. Shrewdly and calculatingly, the serpent asks, "Did God say, 'You shall not eat from any tree in the garden'?" (Gen. 3:1). The serpent casts doubt upon God's word and, more important, on God's intention toward us.

In our psalm today, other people are the ones who say, "There is no help for you in God" (Ps. 3:2). Theirs is the same negative voice as the serpent's, mocking, destructive, and confusing in its intent. "You won't make it six months." "What are you thinking? You can't sell your stock so you can stay home with your sick husband!" "God's not going to provide for you. Who do you think made you sick, if not God?" "No one's going to want to come over and care for Edith for a few hours while you get out and do a little shopping. That's too much to ask of anyone when people are so busy." "There's no way you can fulfill your wish to make a trip to the coast." (You can probably fill in plenty of negative statements you have received. Feel free!)

But like the psalmist, we must seek our inner heart and not be frightened by negative fears rearing their ugly heads. Remember that more often than not, our fears are unfounded. But we must turn and cry out to the Lord; the Lord will hear us and respond by sustaining us.

We can face and survive anything if God is with us. We can lie down and sleep in peace. We can wake again without fear. As the psalmist says, "Deliverance belongs to the Lord," even in death.

PRAYER SUGGESTION

When I was a child, my mom or dad always came to my room to be with me as I said my nightly prayers. Children are comforted by trusting that while they are asleep, God will protect them and everyone they love. The same kind of prayerful trust can comfort adults. God will guard our waking and our sleeping.

Try practicing a Prayer of Release. Focus your mind on releasing—detaching from your thoughts and emotions. Put your thoughts in some peaceful place. In your mind see a place that is beautiful and safe for you. (My favorite image is going to the beach with Jesus.) Go there in your mind and open yourself to being nurtured and sustained. Seek peace. If you wish, accompany your thoughts with relaxing music.

The purpose of the Prayer of Release is to help you let go of frightening thoughts and emotions and to lead you toward inner peace and confidence. Realize that God watches over your waking and your sleeping. No matter what happens, you will be all right.

PRAYER

O Lord, we are besieged by enemies.
Debts and loss come knocking at our door.
Illness and frailty come knocking.
Fear and despair come knocking.
People laugh at us and say, "There is no help for you
in God."
But we know that they are the ones who do not speak
the truth. We trust in you! We cry out to you, for you
rise up to sustain us.
You deliver us from all our enemies.
We can lie down in sleep and wake up again in the
confidence that you are with us. You protect us.
May your name be praised, Lord God,
and may your blessing be upon us. Amen.

WHOM SHALL I FEAR?

The LORD is my light and my salvation;
whom shall I fear?
The LORD is the stronghold of my life;
of whom shall I be afraid?

Psalm 27:1

Rick and his wife were special hospice patients and friends. While receiving hospice care, they worked at living fully as they prepared for Rick's death. They took advantage of everything I offered, and I witnessed their profound courage and love for each other. Being part of their eight-month journey with Hospice Austin was a great gift for me.

Rick was forty-nine years old when he was diagnosed with brain cancer. At our second meeting, Rick began to examine his beliefs about God, life, and death. Like many people his age, Rick had not previously had a reason for searching deep within himself to know exactly what he believed. He had been too busy responding to life to reflect upon it. Now he allowed death to reshape his living.

As we progressed in our journey together, we came to a time when Rick and his wife were no longer able to be wrapped up in living life. Now they had to face the reality that Rick's health was failing, and their lives became more concerned with dying. Understandably, this time was difficult for both of them, and they experienced great fear.

I began using guided meditations to combat their fear. This helped Rick's wife. Initially the guided meditations helped Rick too; however, one day as we got ready to meditate, he made it clear that he did not want to block the fear but to encounter and to embrace it. From then until his death a month or so later, Rick met his fears daily with great courage and eventually died in peace. His wife and I believe that he is in the land of the living, seeing and celebrating the goodness of the Lord. Rick's fear has transformed into joy.

PSALM 27:1-6, 13-14

The LORD is my light and my salvation;
    whom shall I fear?
The LORD is the stronghold of my life;
    of whom shall I be afraid?

When evildoers assail me
    to devour my flesh—
my adversaries and foes—
    they shall stumble and fall.

Though an army encamp against me,
    my heart shall not fear;
though war rise up against me,
    yet I will be confident.

One thing I asked of the LORD,
    that will I seek after:
to live in the house of the LORD
    all the days of my life,
to behold the beauty of the LORD,
    and to inquire in his temple.

For he will hide me in his shelter
    in the day of trouble;
he will conceal me under the cover of his tent;
    he will set me high on a rock.

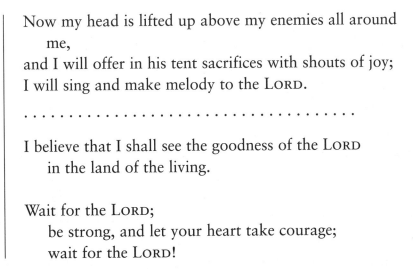

Now my head is lifted up above my enemies all around
    me,
and I will offer in his tent sacrifices with shouts of joy;
I will sing and make melody to the LORD.

. . . .

I believe that I shall see the goodness of the LORD
    in the land of the living.

Wait for the LORD;
    be strong, and let your heart take courage;
    wait for the LORD!

The opening words from Psalm 27 have saved my life on several occasions; such was the case last May. The previous summer I had already made one of the biggest moves in my life—I had left pastoring local churches in Oklahoma and moved to the Austin, Texas, area. I came to Austin without a job but with a calling and vision to initiate Whispering Hope Ministries for Healing and Wholeness. Since I had already experienced significant change in every area of my life, my world was shaken when ten months later I found myself in a time of unexpected transition and change. (Actually, I had a premonition of this change, which made it all the more unsettling.) Like a rose bush being pruned so that it can bring forth new growth, so my life was being pruned again.

Fear is a challenging emotion. It makes us guarded, weary, apprehensive. Fear can cause us to become overly reactive, so we need to be calmed and reassured that everything is going to be all right. I am not generally a fearful person, but last May I experienced moments of great fear about the unknown and the frailty of life. This kind of existential fear shakes you to your roots. I needed an anchor for my faith, so I turned to God for inspiration.

My fear literally drove me straight to Psalm 27. As I read the psalm, it spoke deeply to my heart. Normally I do not have any enemies; no army surrounds me. But on this day I had enemies, and it seemed that an army had camped around me. Psalm 27 became my psalm and my anchor to God. I sang songs and felt the Holy Spirit's presence uplifting me. I made a commitment to read a psalm each day as a way of fighting my apprehension and fear. I figured that my meditative reading would give God an easy way to communicate with me daily, should God so choose.

Twenty-six days later this book, *Abiding Hope,* sprang to life within me. I do not believe the inspiration would have happened if I hadn't been reading and praying the Psalms daily. They were the very ground, the fertile soil, for the birthing of this book. It seems that not only did my fear drive me to the Psalms, but once I was there, the Psalms gave my life new direction. Ironically, the very changes that brought fear also brought the joy of new life and ultimately gave me the time and space I needed to write.

Illness and loss are real sources of fear and apprehension; illness literally devours our flesh. But God's power can lift us above our enemies and free us from our fears. Like Rick, I faced my fears, called on my faith, clung to my hope for dear life, and found joy in the end.

The best answer to "Whom shall I fear?" is "No one." Trust and rest in the shelter of the Most High. May your fears be transformed into joys.

PRAYER SUGGESTION

Guided imagery in prayer can powerfully reinforce our faith and reduce our fears. One of the meditations I used with Rick and his wife was designed to combat fear. Perhaps this exercise will also help you.

Start by relaxing your body. Tense your muscles, hold the tension for a moment, and then release it. Start at the top of your head and work your way down to your feet. Increase your mental relaxation by imagining in your mind's eye that you are going down an escalator. Ride down two or three sets of escalators.

When you arrive at the bottom (or when relaxed), visualize a room that reflects your tastes. See a door, behind which lurks fear. Ask God for help and then seal the doorway. You can board it up, spread concrete over it, or do whatever you need to do to keep the fear out. Rest in the trust that God will reinforce your barriers and will deliver you from your fears.

Then imagine warm, healing light filling the room. When you are ready, open your eyes.

PRAYER

The Lord is our light and our salvation;
whom shall we fear?
The Lord is the stronghold of our lives;
of whom shall we be afraid?
Though disease and fear seek to devour us,
nonetheless our hearts shall not fear.
For we have made you our dwelling place;
in you we rest secure.
Our fears will give way to joy,
and we will dwell in your tents forever and ever. Amen.

THE VALUE
OF OUR FEELINGS

I am poured out like water, and all my bones are out of joint;
my heart is like wax; it is melted within my breast;
my mouth is dried up like a potsherd, and my tongue sticks to my jaws;
you lay me in the dust of death.

Psalm 22:14-15

I am still amazed when ill people tell me that families, friends, or hired helpers complain when they express feelings of loss and grief. Such is the case for Marian. Struggling to overcome cancer, she received an even harsher blow when she developed neuropathy, a condition where her hands and feet were progressively deprived of feeling. A tingling sensation replaced Marian's normal neural feelings. She can no longer walk; in fact, she spent six weeks in a cast after trying to walk. A great lover of crafts, Marian has eighteen unfinished Saint Nicholas dolls that she was planning to finish for Christmas. But because she can no longer use her hands, the dolls will remain unfinished.

The good news is that Marian's cancer is inactive enough that she is no longer "hospice appropriate"—it appears that cancer will not take her life within the next six months. Therefore, Hospice Austin is discharging her from our program. When I visited Marian today, I expected to find her pleased that her cancer is less active. Instead I found a woman who didn't understand why she is being discharged.

Bedridden with useless hands and feet, Marian believes she needs and deserves our services. In her misunderstanding, she was feeling hurt that we did not consider her "worthy" of our help. After I explained that hospice services anticipate that a terminal disease will finish its course within six months,

Marian was able to see that her discharge is good news. She went on to tell me that she will deeply miss our visits because I am the only person with whom she feels safe sharing her feelings.

Marian told me that her hired sitter complained whenever Marian talked about losing the use of her hands. The sitter made a comment that led Marian to believe that the sitter did not want to hear about her condition anymore, so Marian obliged and kept silent. Some time later Marian pointed out to the sitter that she (Marian) hadn't said anything for a long time. The sitter exclaimed, "I can't stand to hear you complain when there's nothing I can do to improve your situation."

Sometimes the people closest to us can't deal with our illness, so they don't. They feel powerless, as if our complaints and expressions point out their failure. But this is unfair to the person who suffers. Both the ill person and the caregiver are in difficult situations. Both individuals' feelings are valid, and both have a right to express their feelings. Few of us like a whiner; yet it is important to distinguish whining from genuine expressions of grief, loss, and lack of control.

Some people feel that expressing negative emotions toward God is wrong or sacrilegious. It is as though we must always wear a mask when addressing God. This idea probably grows in part out of society's pressure on us to compartmentalize ourselves. For instance, few of us get to take our soul and spirit to work with us. Similarly, we teach boys that it is effeminate to cry, and we urge them to repress such emotions.

But in dealing with our emotions and feelings, we must ask ourselves, is it healthy to compartmentalize them? Should we try to ignore or suppress our emotions? What will we gain and what will we sacrifice? If our feelings have value, is there not also value in expressing them?

Since God created us with emotions, is it not valid that we express our feelings to God and to other human beings? Even Jesus cried out in his despair while hanging on the cross, "My God, my God, why have you forsaken me?" (Matt. 27:46). Many people think that Jesus quoted Psalm 22 to express his heart's desperation. That makes sense when you read other parts of the psalm that refer to casting lots for clothing and being poured out like water. Let's look at the psalm.

PSALM 22:1-19, 22-24, 29-31

My God, my God, why have you forsaken me?
Why are you so far from helping me, from the words
    of my groaning?

O my God, I cry by day, but you do not answer;
    and by night, but find no rest.

Yet you are holy, enthroned on the praises of Israel.
In you our ancestors trusted; they trusted, and you
    delivered them.
To you they cried, and were saved;
    in you they trusted, and were not put to shame.

But I am a worm, and not human;
    scorned by others, and despised by the people.
All who see me mock at me; they make mouths at me,
    they shake their heads; "Commit your cause to the
    LORD; let him deliver—let him rescue the one in whom
    he delights!"

Yet it was you who took me from the womb;
    you kept me safe on my mother's breast.
On you I was cast from my birth,
    and since my mother bore me you have been my God.

Do not be far from me,
    for trouble is near and there is no one to help.
Many bulls encircle me,

strong bulls of Bashan surround me;
they open wide their mouths at me, like a ravening and
    roaring lion.

I am poured out like water, and all my bones are out of joint;
    my heart is like wax; it is melted within my breast;
my mouth is dried up like a potsherd, and my tongue sticks
    to my jaws; you lay me in the dust of death.

For dogs are all around me; a company of evildoers encircles
    me.
My hands and feet have shriveled; I can count all my
    bones.
They stare and gloat over me; they divide my clothes among
    themselves, and for my clothing they cast lots.

But you, O Lord, do not be far away!
O my help, come quickly to my aid!

. . . .

I will tell of your name to my brothers and sisters;
    in the midst of the congregation I will praise you:
You who fear the Lord, praise him!
All you offspring of Jacob, glorify him;
    stand in awe of him, all you offspring of Israel!
For he did not despise or abhor the affliction of the
    afflicted; he did not hide his face from me, but heard
    when I cried to him.

. . . .

To him, indeed, shall all who sleep in the earth bow down;
    before him shall bow all who go down to the dust,
    and I shall live for him.

> Posterity will serve him; future generations will be told
>   about the Lord,
> and proclaim his deliverance to a people yet unborn,
>   saying that he has done it.

What an incredibly powerful psalm of grief and trust. The psalmist feels devastated—he is poured out like water; his bones are out of joint; his heart is like wax; he lies in the dust of death. People wasting away from cancer and other illnesses certainly understand this psalm's vivid descriptions.

Illness and dying are hard. They are life changing. Our reactions are real and deserve to be heard honestly. There is value in our fear, apprehension, anger, and revulsion.

Likewise, caring for a terminally ill person is trying. There is merit and truth in our stress, resentment, and sense of being overwhelmed.[1] Certainly God does not begrudge us our feelings or expect us not to feel. After all, the Creator gave us our emotions. God never said that dying was easy—only that God is present with us to give us the grace and strength we need.

No matter what our physical or emotional condition is, God is not put off or repulsed. Rather than despise or abhor our affliction, the Holy One loves us. Sometimes, though, it seems that God's face is hidden from us.

Ruthie was in a pain crisis when she went to our inpatient unit. Her pain was not just physical; she also carried a heavy burden of emotional and spiritual pain. In opening up to me, she tentatively exclaimed, "Sometimes I don't feel God close to me." I said, "That's true for me too."

Ruthie went on to describe the intense emotional and spiritual pain she felt because of her employer's rejection following her illness. Cancer was rampant in Ruthie's family, so she expected to die of it, even at the early age of fifty-five. But why did God let her employer betray her?

That afternoon Ruthie poured out her heart to me. My spirit cried with her as I grieved with her over her employer's unkind actions. We talked about where God was in her circumstances. The depth of sharing between us touched me. Ruthie died two days later. The unexpected timing of her death stunned me, but I was grateful that our discussion had lightened her heart's burden. She had been unable to talk to her family about her feelings. I was blessed that she chose to share them with me.

We all need people we can trust with our feelings, people who will listen to us and be with us in our pain. God did not create us to be islands unto ourselves but to enjoy relationships with God and one another. Whether you are the ill person or caregiver, your feelings have value and worth. May you find trustworthy people to whom you can pour out your heart.

Don't be afraid to express your feelings to God, for the Compassionate One will not despise or abhor you. God will not turn away from you; instead God will hear and, above all others, will understand.

PRAYER SUGGESTION

Sit calmly and quietly for several minutes. With whom can you speak your heart and mind? Give thanks for those persons. Do you know individuals whose feelings you can validate? Seek opportunities to let them share feelings as they choose. Be aware of the value of feelings, and seek healthy ways to express them.

PRAYER

O God of us all, you created us with bodies, souls,
*   and spirits.*
You gave us feelings and emotions so that we might more
*   fully experience life.*
Yet, at times our hearts are crushed within us. We are
*   broken and we hurt.*
We are frightened by our vulnerability and have no place
*   to put our fears.*
We need people and places to honestly pour out our souls.
Please validate our feelings by giving us trustworthy people
*   with whom to share.*

Help us to release our concerns.
Lighten our burdens, for it is in your holy name that we
    pray. Amen.

Be Aware
of Your Feelings

Save me, O Lord, from my enemies;
I have fled to you for refuge.
Teach me to do your will, for you are my God.
Let your good spirit lead me on a level path.

Psalm 143:8

Every now and then, when I get out of bed in the morning I am out of sorts with the world and with myself. Have you ever felt this way? I don't really know why I am out of sorts; I just am. Perhaps my dreams or some unconscious memory associated with the calendar date caused the funk, but it seems that I just awaken and am not in a good mood.

When these days occur, I have two choices: I can go into the day unaware of why I feel the way I do and hope that my mood will improve, or I can sit prayerfully and record my thoughts and feelings in my journal. If I do the former, I may or may not get better that day. If I do the latter, I always get in touch with my feelings and discover what troubles me.

One of the powers of keeping a journal is that it enlightens us about ourselves. We humans are complex creatures with both a conscious and an unconscious mind. Psychologists tell us that most of our activity is unconscious, such as the thoughts that control our automatic body functions. Sometimes we search our mind, our unconscious, for a word or memory. As we talk, words usually just appear from our unconscious. That is one reason we are taught to "think before you speak"—in other words, know what you are going to say before you say it. Practicing this maxim can save a person a lot of heartache.

To grow emotionally, we must know ourselves well. We will repeat the same emotions and reactions to situations until we are able to think them through. When we understand why we feel a certain way, part of that negative energy dissipates, and we find ourselves at a vantage point where we can change our feelings. Let me clarify the difference between *reacting* and *responding*.

A reaction follows an action. For example, if you hit me in the right place on my knee, my leg will kick up. If you say something hateful to me, I may feel hurt and react by saying something hateful back. On the other hand, if you are a doctor, I may respond to your hitting me on the knee with relief that my nerves are functioning as they should. If you are a friend acting silly, I may respond by trying to hit your knee or by wrestling you to the floor.

In contrast to a reaction, *a response can involve reflection and freedom.* If you say something hateful to me, I may feel hurt, but I can reflect on why you said it and respond accordingly. Perhaps you said it because you are angry about being ill, and I am the closest person against whom you can lash out. I can choose not to respond negatively and simply deal with my hurt feelings, or I might say, "I know you don't really mean that, so I'm not going to take it personally." Knowing yourself and others is the key to responding in positive ways rather than just reacting.

PSALM 143

Hear my prayer, O LORD;
    give ear to my supplications in your faithfulness;
    answer me in your righteousness.

Do not enter into judgment with your servant,
    for no one living is righteous before you.

For the enemy has pursued me, crushing my life to
    the ground,
making me sit in darkness like those long dead.

Therefore my spirit faints within me;
  my heart within me is appalled.

I remember the days of old,
  I think about all your deeds,
  I meditate on the works of your hands.
I stretch out my hands to you;
  my soul thirsts for you like a parched land.

Answer me quickly, O LORD; my spirit fails.
Do not hide your face from me,
  or I shall be like those who go down to the Pit.
Let me hear of your steadfast love in the morning,
  for in you I put my trust.
Teach me the way I should go, for to you I lift up my soul.

Save me, O LORD, from my enemies;
  I have fled to you for refuge.
Teach me to do your will, for you are my God.
Let your good spirit lead me on a level path.

For your name's sake, O LORD, preserve my life.
  In your righteousness bring me out of trouble.
In your steadfast love cut off my enemies,
  and destroy all my adversaries, for I am your servant.

Sometimes we are our own worst enemies. That is why it is important to get in touch with our feelings if we can. (Sometimes illness may preclude that.) Giving prayerful attention to ourselves, especially though journaling, gets the words and ideas "out there" where we can deal with them. We can approach this task by asking God to enlighten us. The Holy Spirit can lead us not only to understand ourselves and others but also to discern the best responses for our situation.

To walk on a "level path" means that we make steady progress without the roller-coaster emotions of an unreflected life. This is not a state at which we arrive and stay forever. We may have to daily seek the guidance and strength to walk on level ground, but it is a path with greater consistency.

Ralph and his wife lived rather private lives until she developed advanced cancer. Then their home became a hotel to relatives who traveled long distances to be with them and to aid them at this difficult time. The loss of privacy was hard for Ralph. At times he reacted by wishing that everyone would go home and that the life he had known would be restored. However, when he thought through the situation, he realized their lives would never be the same. His wife's illness was terminal, and she would soon die.

I encouraged Ralph to spend time reflecting and journaling about their predicament. By doing this, he came to see that the presence of family was good for his wife. He responded by looking for ways to adapt to the situation. He went golfing alone in the early morning. This activity provided him with an outing, solitude, and time to think. A disciplined man, Ralph kept to himself his discomfort at everyone's presence, and he worked to change his feelings. By the last week of his wife's life, Ralph was able to receive the gift of her family's presence and help in a way that he could not before.

If Ralph had not recognized his feelings, he might have acted in ways he later would have regretted—he might have done something that could harm his relationship with his in-laws or affect the care of his wife. Also, he might not have sought outlets for releasing his frustration and nervousness at living with a houseful of people. While prayerful reflection was not originally a natural path for Ralph, it became a way for him to walk a level path on rough, uneven terrain. Thank goodness Ralph took the path he did, for his sake and his family's.

PRAYER SUGGESTION

If you do not already keep a journal, I recommend that you begin this practice. Journaling can help you learn more about yourself, and it allows you to honestly express your thoughts and feelings. Share it with others only as you choose. You need freedom to express yourself without having to worry about what others think.

I also encourage you to make an emotional time line related to your illness (or your loved one's illness if you are a caregiver). Along this time line, note feelings such as shock, anger, frustration, relief, joy. Can you see a pattern? What helped you move from one mood to another? How might your future path look, now that you know more about yourself?

PRAYER

Creating God, you made us complex and wondrous
    creatures.
You gave us emotions so we can feel life.
Sometimes our feelings are wonderful and we don't
    want them to stop.
But at other times, they are disruptive and disturbing.
Guide us, O great God, not just to react to the
    situations around us, but to respond with
    wisdom and love.
Help us to know ourselves.
Help us to seek your Spirit's guidance,
    both to enlighten us and to guide us on level
    paths.
In your name we pray. Amen.

POWER BELONGS TO GOD

Once God has spoken;
twice have I heard this:
that power belongs to God,
and steadfast love belongs to you, O LORD.
For you repay to all according to their work.
Psalm 62:11-12

As living organisms, human beings begin from two simple cells and progress through a definite sequence of physical development. Unless something interrupts our natural progression, we grow physically from conception to babyhood, toddlerhood, childhood, adolescence, young adulthood, middle age, old age, and finally death.

While our bodies follow this progression, whether or not we want them to, our emotions and spirits do not naturally mature and grow. Just because I am fifty or seventy years old does not mean that I have a more mature view of God than I did at seventeen or even seven years of age. Yes, it is true that life teaches us all, and to a certain extent we grow and mature as the years pass. Similarly, our brains develop during childhood and adolescence, making us capable of more advanced ways of thinking and understanding. However, unless as adults we reflect upon the concepts we learned as children, our attitudes can remain much the same for the rest of our lives.

Perhaps no attitude that we hold from childhood requires more reeducation than our understanding of God. Children are taught simple concepts of God because they cannot think abstractly. They develop mental pictures of God from the stories they hear—stories like Abraham's near-sacrifice of Isaac, the destruction of the Tower of Babel, and the saving of Noah and the animals in the midst of the Flood. As a result, children (and sometimes adults) may view God as another Santa Claus—someone who gives them what they want—or as a judge who punishes them for all their wrong actions.

Illness often gives us pause to reassess our lives—to examine what we truly believe about God and the meaning of life. If we are wise caregivers, watching a loved one go through illness can cause us to do the same soul-searching. The writer of Psalm 62 had searched his soul and knew who God was. The psalm challenges us to do the same.

PSALM 62:5-8, 11-12

For God alone my soul waits in silence,
    for my hope is from him.
He alone is my rock and my salvation,
    my fortress; I shall not be shaken.
On God rests my deliverance and my honor;
    my mighty rock, my refuge is in God.

Trust in him at all times, O people;
    pour out your heart before him;
God is a refuge for us.

. . . .

Once God has spoken;
    twice have I heard this:
that power belongs to God,
    and steadfast love belongs to you, O Lord.
For you repay to all according to their work.

I experienced a dramatic conversion as an adult. Raised as a Roman Catholic, I attended parochial schools for twelve years. As a child I greatly loved God, but my faith was devastated during adolescence, and I wandered spiritually for many years. My concept of God grew out of my thinking and rationalizations rather than coming from any understanding of the Creator of all life.

One of the most significant factors in reassessing my life and redirecting it toward God was an unexplained illness at age thirty-six. Another factor was a certain person God placed in my life at work. Jerry was a born-again Christian, and over several years we discussed God, Jesus, and faith extensively and sometimes heatedly. I saw the power of his faith and wanted it for myself. Eventually I decided such faith was worth whatever it cost.

My transformation occurred over a period of sixteen months. The change began in earnest with my commitment to read and study the Bible so that I could learn about God and the meaning of being a Christian. In my usual intense way I joined three Bible studies! I gained a great deal of understanding about God and made many wonderful Christian friends, but still my heart had an emptiness that possessions, accomplishments, and people could not fill. After sixteen months of study, I had run into a brick wall spiritually. Something had to change—and that something was me. On November 5, 1987, I finally surrendered control of my life to God. I allowed God into parts of my life that had previously been off limits.

One week later I attended a women's retreat that changed my life forever because I experienced God's power in a real and personal way. A group of women invited me to visit with them. As I stepped into the doorway of the lodge room, this voice inside me (using my own voice) said, "Ann, sit down next to the woman on the bed and give her your pocket cross." I probably stood in the doorway for a full three minutes, arguing with God. Oh, I was more than willing to give up my silver cross, for I had learned that everything belongs to God. The problem was, I wanted to choose the person to whom I would give it! My old issue of control was at work again.

Finally, I relented and sat next to a woman I had never met. As I handed her my cross, I told her I felt strongly compelled to do so. She began crying. I learned later that her father was a minister, and when she was a child, he had given her a pocket cross. He had also sexually abused her. Because of his abuse and Christians' incorrect and often excessive perception of God as a male, she could not accept God as a reality in her life.

Through my obedient actions this woman knew that God was reaching out to her, offering hope and healing. Her life would never be the same, nor would mine. God's power had been manifested to me. God had spoken to me and used sinful, inadequate *me* to touch the life of another with healing. How awesome! That event was the definitive change in my life and in my relationship to everyone and everything around me.

Power indeed belongs to God, and steadfast love belongs to the Lord, as Psalm 62 says. God alone is our rock and salvation, our fortress and refuge. We can trust God at all times—good and bad—with our pains and our joys. We can open our hearts and lives to God's loving presence. What the psalmist knows, we too can know. But make no mistake about it: Only God is really God. We cannot control the Almighty, but we can open ourselves to God's power in our lives. If we genuinely do this, no matter what our condition, our lives will no longer be the same. They will be immeasurably improved.

The psalmist's words in verse 12 are sobering: "For you repay to all according to their work." These words are not meant as a threat to be used against us but rather as a statement of reality. Our work is to seek God and open ourselves to God's power and presence in our lives. If we are unwilling to trust and open ourselves to God, the Holy Spirit is restricted in working in our situations. But if we are willing to risk being open, then God's Spirit can move in and bring us peace and joy beyond human comprehension. The choice is ours. I am so glad I chose to surrender, for I have discovered that power truly belongs to God.

PRAYER SUGGESTION

Spend time reflecting and journaling on your relationship with God. When, where, and how did you first learn about God? Have your understandings come mostly from what someone else taught you? When have you spent time as an adult learning and reflecting on who God is? In what ways is God a power in your life? When have you experienced times of knowing or feeling God's power in your circumstances?

PRAYER

O God of power and love, come and touch our lives.
Touch our hearts and warm them with your caring.
Touch our souls and inspire them with your wisdom.
Touch our bodies and heal them with your wholeness.
Be real to us. Be to us a rock and fortress.
Help us to trust you with all that we are and all that we
have. Amen.

The Power of Prayer

He will not let your foot be moved;
he who keeps you will not slumber.
Psalm 121:3

Twice in my life, I have earned an airline flight voucher. This was my second time. I decided to use the voucher to fly to Oklahoma City to see my dad for Thanksgiving. I booked my flights on Monday night and planned to go by the airport Tuesday morning to redeem my voucher after visiting a patient who lived close to the airport.

My visit with the patient turned out to be relatively short. As I pulled into the airport, my pager went off. It was my sister. As I walked through the airport, she told me that our dad had suffered another stroke and was in the emergency room. I walked up to an airline agent and said, "I had planned to pay for my flight on the eighteenth, but I think I need to fly today instead." While she checked on flight availability, I quickly assessed my week. My schedule called for me to conduct a wedding on Saturday, so I needed to be back by Friday evening, but I could postpone everything else. I booked the flight; it cost $250, and my voucher was worth $275!

I felt stunned. Here I was, in the airport, holding an airline voucher when I learned from my sister that our dad had suffered a stroke. Not only did I feel without a doubt that I needed to go to Oklahoma City, but the circumstances and timing also made me feel God's presence in the midst of our situation. (I say "our" because when God intervenes to support an individual, that support applies to everyone involved in the situation.) Being able to see God's fingerprints in these events encouraged me. Indeed, God empowers us to do things we couldn't do on our own. With God's grace all things become possible.

As I took care of business, packed, and traveled to Oklahoma City, my heart turned to Psalm 121 for the strength to make the journey, face whatever I would find, and do whatever I must to help my dad. Psalm 121 sustained me. It breathes encouragement into our lives.

PSALM 121

I lift up my eyes to the hills—
    from where will my help come?
My help comes from the LORD,
    who made heaven and earth.

He will not let your foot be moved;
    he who keeps you will not slumber.
He who keeps Israel
    will neither slumber nor sleep.

The LORD is your keeper;
    the LORD is your shade at your right hand.
The sun shall not strike you by day,
    nor the moon by night.

The LORD will keep you from all evil;
    he will keep your life.
The LORD will keep your going out and your coming in
    from this time on and forevermore.

Psalm 121 is one of my favorites. It was the second psalm I memorized, and I like to pray it together with the Twenty-third Psalm. Occasionally I reflect upon the truth of the words of this psalm. Is it true that my foot is never moved? Do I never stumble about? Certainly I have spent some time on top of banana peels!

The question is, if my foot indeed is moved at times, does that mean that God's word in Psalm 121 is not true? For instance, if I have a terminal illness,

54

has God let me down? Has the Lord allowed my foot to slip? I don't think so. Death is a part of God's design for life. Death is within God's circumstantial will for all of us; it is within the scope of what God allows to happen to all people. We must look beyond death to God's eternal purposes for us.

God promises us life forevermore. Eternal life will not be life as we imagine but as God ordains. Death is a transition to the next life, the next stage in our journey with the divine. It is uplifting to know that as bad and painful as life can become, difficulty is a part of life; we don't have to face our trials alone. God sustains us, protecting us from all evil. God guards our going out and our coming in. Even death is not final.

As a hospice worker, I have witnessed several fascinating experiences with death. On my first day at our inpatient unit, I was present when a woman died. While visiting with her daughter Katherine, I noticed that the patient was near the end of physical life, so I stayed in the room. Shortly after that she breathed her last. As Katherine gently cried, she remarked that she was disappointed not to see her mother's spirit leave her. When I asked what she meant, she explained that once before she had seen someone die—her sister, Sandra. When Sandra died, Katherine saw Sandra's spirit rise up out of her body. Katherine assumed that this happened at all deaths. I told her that perhaps because her sister died at an unnatural time in life, God allowed her to see Sandra's spirit in order to sustain her through the tragic loss.

If you believe in life after death, you can pray this psalm as a source of courage and confidence. Employ the power of prayer by abandoning yourself to trust God's present and future plans for you and for those you love.

Lift up your eyes to the hills—from where shall your help come? It will come from the Lord, who made heaven and earth. It will come from the One who guards your coming in and going out now and forever. Thanks be to God!

PRAYER SUGGESTION

Keep a copy of Psalm 121 with you. You can write it down, copy it, or keep a Bible nearby. Read the psalm frequently during the day. Let it penetrate the center of your being with encouragement.

PRAYER

O Lord of heaven and earth, when we are feeling low or
  cast down, lift up our hearts as we lift up our eyes
  to you.
Do not let our feet trip.
Do not let enemies trouble our hearts.
Do not let us be struck by day or by night, for you are
  our keeper.
You protect us from all evil. You guard us now and
  always. Amen.

GOD IS MY HELPER

But surely, God is my helper;
the LORD is the upholder of my life.
He will repay my enemies for their evil.
In your faithfulness, put an end to them.
Psalm 54:4-5

Sometimes life deals us a dirty blow. At times even our friends and families betray us. The resulting anger and devastation can eat away at us like a cancer. When we internalize negative emotions and cannot release them, poor health may result. Scarlet taught me much about the effect of negative emotions.

Scarlet came from a prominent, wealthy family but gave up that lifestyle to marry the man she loved and to live in his small hometown. Their marriage seems to have been happy, and they are blessed with five children who live close enough to be a strong support.

Scarlet's problems came from her family of origin. Her father and oldest brother were in the oil business. When her father died, the brother refused to follow the will and divide the estate among the living siblings. The ensuing squabble produced great heartache for Scarlet and two of her siblings. Even though the father had died a few years ago, his will was still unresolved. Each child hired a certified public accountant to investigate the business records and other information.

I visited Scarlet one day shortly after the CPA left. With great passion she told me, "I don't want to spend what energy I have left on money. It's already broken my health and my sister's and brother's." As Scarlet pointed out, she had lived without money all these years; getting it at the end of her life was not important to her. What devastated Scarlet, and understandably so, was her oldest brother's total betrayal, insensitivity, and cruelty.

Is Scarlet doomed to die filled with disappointment, pain, and anger? Is there any help for her?

When disappointments affect our life, is there help for us? Psalm 54 can guide us here.

PSALM 54:1-2, 4-7

Save me, O God, by your name,
and vindicate me by your might.
Hear my prayer, O God;
give ear to the words of my mouth.

. . . .

But surely, God is my helper;
the LORD is the upholder of my life.
He will repay my enemies for their evil.
In your faithfulness, put an end to them.

With a freewill offering I will sacrifice to you;
I will give thanks to your name, O LORD, for it is good.
For he has delivered me from every trouble,
and my eye has looked in triumph on my enemies.

What image comes to mind when you think of the word *helper?* For me, the ideal helper would assist in every situation of need. The psalmist's image of God as the helper who upholds our lives works well for me. When I say that God helps my every need, remember that God uses many sources and resources to meet our needs, from divine inspiration to the hands and feet of other people.

As human beings, we greatly need nurture. When sea turtle eggs hatch, the young immediately make their way out to sea. But we humans require spiritual, emotional, physical, and relational care and nurture. We need a helper all the days of our life. It is really an awe-inspiring thought to think that God, the Creator of all, is our helper and the One who upholds each of our lives.

Illness and caregiving can make us feel trapped and bound by chains. How would you feel if you were swimming in a lake and suddenly became tangled in seaweed? Frightened, no doubt. Life in the shadow of death can feel like being caught in seaweed. Negative thoughts, doubts, fears, and wounds can ensnare our minds. If we do not get free of them, they can drown us. We need a helper to deliver us from every trouble. We need God, because only God is our ultimate and complete helper.

The psalmist is angry. He has enemies and does not hesitate to ask God to put an end to them. As Christians we are called to entrust our enemies to God's judgment. "Kill them" can be our prayer, but to have peace we must try to work through our pain—if not to forgiveness, then at least to liberation. We must trust in God's perfect judgment and compassion.

There is no justification for the damage Scarlet's oldest brother has inflicted on his family. He has exhibited greed, haughtiness, pride, and disobedience. Each failing is a major sin in God's eyes. But only God can judge him and repay him according to the full information that only God knows.

Scarlet is deeply injured. She will probably go to her grave with these wounds, yet she realizes the entrapment and destructiveness of the situation. She is wise to desire not to spend her final energies on fighting her brother about money. At this point, all the money in the world cannot undo the pain she has endured. Fortunately Scarlet has more important priorities. Through her faith she is seeking to move beyond her pain and hurt and to break free of their entanglements.

I hope that by listening and offering emotional support and counsel, I have served as one of God's helpers for Scarlet. Perhaps you can be God's helper by aiding someone in breaking free of the seaweed that engulfs and threatens to drown him or her. Or perhaps you need a helper to be able to work through your own entanglements. If so, offer a prayer to God and be on the alert for help to come to your aid. The help may not undo what has been done to you, but it can prevent your being destroyed by it. Truly the Lord is our helper and the upholder of our lives. Thanks be to God!

Today I invite you to examine your life for areas in which negative emotions toward another person are zapping your energy. Offer a prayer to God, seeking God's help for dealing with the negative emotions.

Prayer

God of power and strength, we need you.
We need you to save us.
O God, our helper in all ages, please be near us,
*   for we are hurt and need your healing.*
Release us from the bonds that threaten to weigh us down
*   and drown us.*
Put an end to our suffering, and vindicate us by your
*   power and might.*
You are our helper; how blessed we are! Amen.

Even though I walk through
the valley of the shadow of death,
I fear no evil;
for you are with me;
your . . . staff . . . comfort[s] me.

Psalm 23:4

PART TWO | The Shepherd's Staff Guides Us

Stir Yourself to Faithfulness

Awake, my soul!
Awake, O harp and lyre!
I will awake the dawn.
Psalm 57:8

I had made an appointment to meet with Virginia and her husband on Wednesday. Though they had been with Hospice Austin for a month, I had not met them. They had recently moved to their daughter's home, north of Austin, and I was part of a new team of hospice workers assigned to them. On Monday when I picked up my voice mail from the weekend on-call staff, I discovered that Virginia's husband had suffered a serious bleeding episode on Sunday, and Virginia had requested a spiritual care visit as soon as possible. I rearranged my schedule and arrived at their house around 11:30 A.M.

When she met me at the door, Virginia was so overwrought that I thought her husband had just died. As it turned out, he was upstairs asleep. Virginia had just gone over the edge, freaking out from the circumstances of her life. Certainly she had many reasons to feel overwhelmed by fear and grief. Her husband had been the top salesperson for his company. At age fifty-two he had made a great deal of money but had spent it as quickly as he had made it. Then a fatal disease had suddenly struck him, and eventually he and Virginia went bankrupt. They lost their home; in fact, they lost every material possession except their clothes and a car. Their destitution forced them to move to Texas to get help from relatives. Initially they moved in with another family member, but that arrangement had not worked well. Now they were staying at their daughter's home until his death.

63

Virginia is ten years older than her husband. Not only had she lost her possessions and the immediate support of her friends, but now she was also losing her husband. How would she survive? How could she survive? She had no work history, skills, or training. In the face of overwhelming tragedies, Virginia desperately needed a shelter to provide her some sense of security, peace, and hope.

When circumstances threaten to overwhelm you, how do you respond? How do you shake yourself out of fear and grief and stir yourself toward what gives you peace, hope, and security? All of us will face these challenges in our lives. It is never too early to be ready to answer to these questions.

PSALM 57:1-3, 7-8

Be merciful to me, O God, be merciful to me,
>   for in you my soul takes refuge;
in the shadow of your wings I will take refuge,
>   until the destroying storms pass by.
I cry to God Most High,
>   to God who fulfills his purpose for me.
He will send from heaven and save me,
>   he will put to shame those who trample on me.
God will send forth his steadfast love and his faithfulness.

. . . .

My heart is steadfast, O God,
>   my heart is steadfast.
I will sing and make melody.
>   Awake, my soul!
Awake, O harp and lyre!
>   I will awake the dawn.

Illness disrupts our normal lives. To borrow the psalmist's imagery, illness brings destructive storms—storms that destroy, uproot, and permanently change the face of our lives. Certainly for Virginia, the storms of illness took her home, her familiar surroundings, her possessions, her husband, her security, her friends, and her way of life. What could she do in the face of such destruction? Where could she find refuge and help?

God is the shelter and refuge for persons of faith. In the shadow of God's wings, we will find the protection we need from life's storms. In God we find security, peace, and hope. The writer of Psalm 57 is experiencing destruction in his life; he sounds as if he is also experiencing the slumber of a person overwhelmed by destroying storms. The psalm begins with a cry for mercy. The psalmist clings to God, recalling God's steadfast love and faithfulness. The memory of who God is and what God can do stirs the embers of his faith. He calls forth to his own soul, "Awake, my soul! / Awake, O harp and lyre!"

The harp and lyre symbolize expressions of praise and thanksgiving. The psalmist tells himself to wake up, to stir up his trust in God. He reminds himself to respond to his threats with steadfast faith, with praise and thanksgiving, for the One who loves him will faithfully come to his aid.

In fact, not only will our psalmist awaken his faith, but also he will awaken the dawn. In other words, his faith will awaken the dawn of help and change, the new light that follows storms. In his faith the psalmist finds great hope. He now has a course of action to survive the destructive storms until they pass by.

That morning I was with Virginia, she was beside herself with fear and grief. Her daughter and I talked with her for several hours. We gave her space and time to express her grief and fears, and then we began to search for pathways to shelter for Virginia where she could find refuge from her storms. I examined with her some areas where she already had faith. Building on that, we looked at a few practices that might stir up the embers of Virginia's slumbering faith. One of the first places we turned was to the Psalms. We found a simple verse or two that she could memorize and repeat to herself as needed. We also discussed meditative prayer, and I encouraged Virginia to envision herself in the sheltering wings of God's safety.

Part of the process of awakening the soul is awakening to the life that surrounds us. We *can* break free of the slumber induced by fear and grief. To do this, we may need to grasp anything around us that awakens us, whether it be

God, family, nature, friends, church, therapy, books, or hospice workers. God is present in all of these things. We must awaken to possibilities that encourage hope, security, and peace. One of the beauties of faith is the peace it provides in the midst of storms; it allows us to endure and to survive situations that might otherwise destroy us. God's peace is manifested in serenity despite circumstances that dictate chaos and fear. We may not be able to explain this serenity, but we can certainly experience it and give thanks and praise for it.

Virginia's faith had been inactive for a long time, and she would not easily find a pathway to shelter. We contacted her daughter's doctor, who prescribed a sedative to help stabilize Virginia. Eventually we convinced her to see a therapist to help address some of her deep, emotional issues. Virginia's daughter, who has strong faith, continues to nurture and to encourage her mother's faith. Together they continue to look for hopeful paths and shelter until the destroying storms pass.

In what areas of your life does your faith need to be awakened from its slumber? May you be stirred to steadfast faithfulness. May your faith be reawakened.

Prayer Suggestion

Think of a time in your past when storms threatened to destroy your life. How did God help pull you through that situation? How has God used family members or friends to help stir your faith? Pinpoint what helped you through trials; then let the memory of what God has done for you in the past strengthen you now. Allow that remembrance to stir up the flames of your faith today.

Prayer

Gracious God, we are only humans, frail and vulnerable.
When the storms of life attack us, we become easily
frightened. We are overwhelmed. But your faithfulness
is a steady shelter for us.
Help us find the pathways that lead to your refuge. Protect
us beneath the shadow of your wings and keep us safe
from all harm.

God of power and might, speak to the storms to calm them; speak to our hearts to calm us.

Help us to stir up our faith and to sing with gratitude for your steadfast love and safety.

O awake, my soul, my faith! Remember what God has done for you. Awake, my soul, and be stirred to faithfulness!

Trust in the Lord, for God's mercy endures forever.

God will be my refuge and protection.

All thanks and praise belong to you, mighty God! Amen.

A Burden Shared

Cast your burden on the LORD,
and he will sustain you.
Psalm 55:22

The world around us wonderfully teaches spiritual principles. For example, each year I prune my roses so that new, vibrant growth will occur. This principle also applies to life. At times I have to endure pruning so that new life can sprout up.

If we are realistic, we know that we have a limited amount of time, energy, and money. If we invest much time and energy in one direction, we cannot start growing in another area unless we redirect hours and energies from the first. For instance, giving up twenty hours each week at Christopher House, our inpatient facility, allowed me to devote that time to writing this book. If I hadn't redirected those hours, I wouldn't have been able to write a book without undue stress and a longer time frame.

While the pruning principle is simple to understand, the actual process of pruning can be quite painful. Whether you have been let down by a disease attacking your body or your life has been turned upside down and redirected by someone else's needs, your life has been radically pruned. Do the Psalms offer words of hope for you? They certainly do. One of my favorite sources of encouragement is Psalm 55.

PSALM 55:1-8, 16-18, 22

Give ear to my prayer, O God;
   do not hide yourself from my supplication.
Attend to me, and answer me;

I am troubled in my complaint.
I am distraught by the noise of the enemy,
   because of the clamor of the wicked.
For they bring trouble upon me,
   and in anger they cherish enmity against me.

My heart is in anguish within me,
   the terrors of death have fallen upon me.
Fear and trembling come upon me,
   and horror overwhelms me.
And I say, "O that I had wings like a dove!
   I would fly away and be at rest;
truly, I would flee far away;
   I would lodge in the wilderness;
I would hurry to find a shelter for myself
   from the raging wind and tempest."

. . . .

But I call upon God,
   and the LORD will save me.
Evening and morning and at noon
   I utter my complaint and moan,
   and he will hear my voice.
He will redeem me unharmed
   from the battle that I wage,
   for many are arrayed against me.

. . . .

Cast your burden on the LORD,
   and he will sustain you;
he will never permit the righteous to be moved.

When we start tallying our burdens, we can quickly feel overwhelmed. It seems that we go into the dual mode of reacting to circumstances outside our control while trying to keep necessary things afloat—like jobs or caring for children. All the while, our hearts are sinking. The psalmist may well have felt the same. Fortunately for him and for us, his mind focuses on both the problem and the solution; and he decides to make his prayer supplications known to God.

As the psalmist approaches God, requesting that God listen to his prayer, he updates God on what is happening in his life. The psalmist is distraught because enemies are clamoring against him. He would love to escape the situation, to sprout wings and fly away; but since he cannot, he calls out to the Lord for help because he knows that the Lord will save him.

It was painful the year I realized that God wanted me to leave the pastorate and step out in an even more daring leap of faith. Among other things, God asked me to give up the security of financial stability and venture off into unknown ministries in another state. It was a time of grief, joy, and uncertainty. I was on vacation in Florida when I found a mouse pad with a water scene that caught my eyes. The scene included the words *Cast your cares upon Jesus* written with fishing line; the word *Jesus* was cleverly scripted inside the body of a fish-shaped lure. Beneath some coral I saw the scripture reference, Psalm 55:22. Since I needed a mouse pad, I bought this one.

At that time I had no idea that the mouse pad would become an anchor of faith for me in that decisive and demanding year. Can you relate to the psalmist's words, "My heart is in anguish within me, / the terrors of death have fallen upon me. / Fear and trembling come upon me, / and horror overwhelms me"? I certainly can. Uncertainty and change can be terrifying.

Remembering that God wants me to cast my burdens on the Lord was good for me. How awesome it was to realize that I did not have to shoulder my burdens alone! In faith I could give them to the Bearer of burdens and their weight would be lightened. Every time I use my computer, my mouse pad reminds me of this spiritual truth.

When I read Psalm 55:22 in my Bible, I noticed a footnote explaining that the Hebrew can also be translated, "Cast what he has given you on the Lord." I was taken aback, for this translation presented a whole new way of looking at my situation. This translation brought up the issue of where God was in my distress. Where is God in the midst of our illnesses and setbacks? Does God give them to us? Are they the result of sin? Or are they just a part of ordinary life, of the trials and crosses that can come to any of us?

The Jewish understanding of God seems radical to us; according to this view, all things—good and evil—come from God. To Jews, there is only one God, and everything comes from God. Verse 22 supports this understanding of one God from whom all things come.

The Book of Job and the Gospels, however, teach that illness happens for various reasons. Job and Jesus countered the dominant Jewish view, that illness is punishment for sin. Job saw illness as a test. Jesus viewed illness as an opportunity for God's works to be revealed in the ill person's life. (See John 9 for the story of the man born blind.) The key message of Psalm 55:22 is that God desires to carry our burdens for us.

When I experienced Psalm 55:22 as a living word, I realized that not only does God invite me to cast my burdens, whatever they are, on the Lord, but also that even if God places burdens on my shoulders, God is willing to take them back. What a relief to know that God knows what is going on in my life—and that God is present in the midst of it to be a shelter from the raging wind and tempest!

Understanding our own lives and how God acts in them requires us to consult God and let our faith and prayer life guide us. The psalmist did not pray just once. He prayed evening, morning, and at noon. He persevered in prayer for God to act in his life as well as for the ability to turn over his burdens to the Lord. Relinquishing burdens can be hard for those of us who prefer to control our own lives.

God never promised us smooth sailing through life. Storms and winds are a part of every person's life. Death is something we all experience. God promises a caring, loving relationship with us. God promises to be with us and sustain us, and that is saving power! The psalmist writes, "Cast your burden on the LORD, / and he will sustain you." If we can discover how to align ourselves with God and lean on God for sustenance, we will be sustained. This is the promise of scripture.

The psalmist is right; given the chance, I would probably seek first to have the wings of a dove and escape the whole situation by flying away. But when the problem is your body or a person you love, escape is not a possible solution. Thank goodness, sharing the burden is! God will sustain us, no matter what, but we must cast our burdens on the Lord.

The last four days of my mother's life were a nightmare for our family, made bearable only because of the grace of God's sustaining power in our lives. Mother was unconscious, with no bodily functions below the waist. The skin of her ankles and legs was breaking down. I had never experienced death like this with anyone, much less my own mother. My family and I cast our burdens and fears on God, and we were sustained through this four-day ordeal. We offered many prayers, sought signs of God's presence with us, and accepted the people who crossed our paths as being sent by God. God did not let us down.

I am convinced that the Lord of life will sustain you too. Cast your burdens on the Lord, and God will see you through.

Prayer Suggestion

Jesus said, "Come to me, all you that are weary and are carrying heavy burdens, and I will give you rest. Take my yoke upon you, and learn from me; for I am gentle and humble in heart, and you will find rest for your souls. For my yoke is easy, and my burden is light" (Matt. 11:28-30).

What burdens can you release by casting them on the Lord? Spend some time identifying them, and then toss them out on God's sea of life for the Gracious One to carry. Release them and feel yourself freed from the burden of carrying them alone.

Prayer

Gracious and loving God, your power is sufficient;
*   you sustain us in every moment of life.*
Help us to trust you.
Help us to cast our burdens on you and to freely let them go
*   into your capable hands.*
Help us to rest in your peace and hope. Amen.

Who Is God?

Righteousness and justice are the foundation of your throne;
steadfast love and faithfulness go before you.
Happy are the people who know the festal shout,
who walk, O LORD, in the light of your countenance.

Psalm 89:14-15

I met Karen on October 1 after she had been diagnosed with terminal breast cancer. She had undergone treatments, but they had been unsuccessful. A lawyer and devout Episcopalian, Karen was an accomplished woman. One year younger than I, she became one of my main teachers on my own mortality.

When Karen found out that she had lost the battle with cancer, she returned to Austin and bought a small, modest home where she could die. Her mother flew in, and her closest friends gathered to provide the necessary caregiving. Karen's two prayers to God were that she be able to maintain her dignity and that she not linger.

More than any person I have served, Karen intentionally directed her final journey toward God. Her home became a sacred space for her to prepare to meet her Maker. The Creator of life chose to respect Karen's prayers. Three weeks after she came on service with us, she left this world to enter another. Who is God that Karen could be so confident in their meeting? Is it possible to know only a little about God, and yet have it be enough? Let us look to our own hearts and to Psalm 89 for answers.

PSALM 89:1-2, 8, 11-12, 14-18

I will sing of your steadfast love, O LORD, forever;
    with my mouth I will proclaim your faithfulness
    to all generations.

I declare that your steadfast love is established forever;
 your faithfulness is as firm as the heavens.

. . . .

O Lord God of hosts,
 who is as mighty as you, O Lord?
Your faithfulness surrounds you.

. . . .

The heavens are yours, the earth also is yours;
 the world and all that is in it—you have founded them.
The north and the south—you created them.

. . . .

Righteousness and justice are the foundation of your throne;
 steadfast love and faithfulness go before you.
Happy are the people who know the festal shout,
 who walk, O Lord, in the light of your countenance;
they exult in your name all day long,
 and extol your righteousness.
For you are the glory of their strength;
 by your favor our horn is exalted.
For our shield belongs to the Lord,
 our king to the Holy One of Israel.

Have you ever tried to conceptualize God? It's hard. That is why we end up with mental pictures of God as a bearded old man sitting on a throne. One beauty in worshiping Jesus is that we have a human frame of reference for God.

What are God's key attributes? As a child, I learned that God was all-knowing, all-present, and all-powerful. These characteristics describe God's power but tell us nothing about God's heart.

Our psalmist repeatedly mentions two key attributes of God: steadfast love and faithfulness. God's steadfast love is established forever; God's faithfulness is as firm as the heavens. We need not doubt God's faithful, steady love.

The psalmist also identifies righteousness and justice as the foundations of God's throne. The Lord is the One who created heaven and earth and everything within them. Righteousness and justice are fundamental to God's creation. Creation is embedded with God's character, and this character is the rightness by which all else is measured or judged. Justice speaks both about the laws and expressions of God's rightness, as well as about God's judgment. God created the world, and only the Creator knows and understands all that is. Ultimately, all will be judged by God and aligned rightly with God's nature.

How wonderful that God's disposition toward us is love! What is critical is that we walk in the light of God's countenance and know what the psalmist calls the "festal shout"—in other words, that we be worshipful people. God's love becomes real and empowering in our lives only to the extent that we know and experience that love. As we cast our burdens on the Lord, God becomes our source of strength. When we experience this strength and love, we celebrate it and worship God.

I wish I had a dollar for every time someone has said to me that he or she doesn't know how he or she could have survived a particular situation without God and faith in God. If you have trouble recognizing God's love for you, begin simply by looking for places of affirmation in your life. The Creator is present in the creation. God can and does reach out to us in many different ways.

Karen was able to make a spiritual pilgrimage during the final weeks of her life. She sought to meet God, but she did so partially in the presence of the loving caregivers who reflected our Creator's love in their lives. She lived and died in the confidence of God's steadfast love and faithfulness. May we always remember that God is on our side, and may we go forward in the strength of this knowledge.

PRAYER SUGGESTION

Who is God to you? Identify words or images that describe God to you. Do not be frustrated by the inability to "get your hands around" God. God is beyond our comprehension. Be content to know just a little. Strive to live in the awareness that God loves you. This alone will be enough.

PRAYER

God of heaven and earth and everything within them,
Thank goodness you are steadfast love and faithfulness
*   itself!*
Thank goodness you are on our side.
We exalt and praise your name!
For surely your throne is founded on your righteousness,
*   and your love precedes you.*
Happy are the people who know your love!
Help us to experience your love more deeply.
Touch especially those of us who have not yet experienced it.
Help us to know your love and to sing the festal shout.
Be our glory and our strength. Amen.

Attending to Our Relationship with God

Be still, and know that I am God!
Psalm 46:10

I am the Lord your God, who brought you out of the land of Egypt, out of the house of slavery; you shall have no other gods before me" (Exod. 20:2-3). The first commandment seems quite clear. Because God redeemed his people from slavery in Egypt, God claimed first place in their hearts and lives. While we have not literally been delivered from slavery in Egypt, through Christ we are delivered from sin and the finality of death, and we can be delivered from the bondages in our lives by allowing the Holy Spirit to work with us. Because God created us and redeemed us from death and bondage, God rightly claims the throne of our hearts. But what does it mean to love God first? Can we really keep the first commandment?

Rosalie, only fifty-four, was losing her battle with breast cancer. She moved to the Austin area to be near her children. They were a close family, and it was wonderful to witness their love and loyalty. When I visited Rosalie, I found on her couch a rosary, the book *Chicken Soup for the Surviving Soul,* and some prayer cards. We talked about these daily helps that give her strength, encouragement, and wisdom. She also attends church and a support group as often as possible.

Rosalie intentionally grounds herself in God's presence and strength each day by using these various vehicles of prayer. Clearly her power for daily life comes from her relationship with God. This is a correct and necessary priority.

Next, she passionately loves her family and life itself. Rosalie did not always put God first, though. The onset of illness drew her to the Lord with a new fervor. She now realizes that by trying to love God first, she does not love her family less. Rather, she rightly aligns herself with God first so that she becomes empowered to love her family more fully.

We must attend to our relationship with God if we are ever to experience God's power in our lives. To this end, Psalm 46 contains one of the greatest spiritual truths: "Be still and know that I am God!" (Ps. 46:10). Let's look at this passage.

PSALM 46

God is our refuge and strength,
    a very present help in trouble.
Therefore we will not fear,
    though the earth should change,
though the mountains shake in the heart of the sea;
    though its waters roar and foam,
though the mountains tremble with its tumult.

There is a river whose streams make glad the city of God,
    the holy habitation of the Most High.
God is in the midst of the city; it shall not be moved;
God will help it when the morning dawns.
The nations are in an uproar, the kingdoms totter;
    he utters his voice, the earth melts.
The LORD of hosts is with us; the God of Jacob is our refuge.

Come, behold the works of the LORD;
    see what desolations he has brought on the earth.
He makes wars cease to the end of the earth;
    he breaks the bow, and shatters the spear;
    he burns the shields with fire.

> "Be still, and know that I am God!
> I am exalted among the nations,
>   I am exalted in the earth."
> The LORD of hosts is with us;
>   the God of Jacob is our refuge.

Psalm 46 is an unusual psalm because it alludes to the end of time. Within this catastrophic event, God is the psalmist's refuge and strength so that he will not be afraid. Though the world is turned upside down, the psalmist knows that God is always a very present help in times of trouble. There is no need for worry.

The "city of God" is a space and time in which God's righteousness rules. It is the promised place where there are neither tears nor death. Everything else in life may be tottering, but the place where God is present shall not be moved. The result of God's activities leads to peace, where wars end and the bow and spear are destroyed.

The psalmist moves from affirming God as a refuge and strength to speaking of God's holiness and power and the devastating end of time, which will birth peace. In the midst of all this calamitous activity comes the command, "Be still, and know that I am God!" To be attentive to God, we must stop and listen.

Stopping reduces other distractions in our lives. We all have important things to do each day, but it seems we allow urgent but unimportant tasks to drive us. How much of what you do today truly will matter in two years or ten years?

When you talk with someone, how often are you distracted by other thoughts, by rehearsing what you will say in response, or by looking at the person and judging him or her but not listening to his or her words? Most of us have trouble stopping and being still.

We make long lists of things we *must* do. But when a genuine crisis arises, it is amazing how many items on our lists get tossed out the window. In the Psalm 121 meditation I told about my father's stroke. I made flight reservations based on an event, other than my dad's death, that required my return to Austin—a wedding that I was blessed to lead for good friends.

But the wedding wasn't the only item on my calendar that week. I had several important commitments, from seeing my patients and spiritual director, to getting a haircut (for the wedding), to meeting with the women with whom I am involved in retreat ministries and a small group on spirituality in the corporate world. All of these activities were important to me, but compared to my dad's stroke, they were insignificant.

The word from God is "be still." We must stop and create the space to interact with God. The other key is to listen. We are stopped for a purpose: to know God. We must listen to our hearts, the words of scripture, the prayers and lives of others, and the healing power of nature that surrounds us. To know God is to have intimate knowledge of God. To know God is to have not just head knowledge but also life experience. We must stop, listen, and hear.

The Gospel of Luke tells the wonderful story of Jesus coming to stay with Martha and Mary. On this particular visit, Mary is sitting and listening to Jesus' teaching, an unusual thing for a woman to do. Martha complains to the Lord and asks him to tell Mary to help her with her tasks. Jesus responds, "Martha, Martha, you are worried and distracted by many things; there is need of only one thing. Mary has chosen the better part, which will not be taken away from her" (Luke 10:41-42).

In this case, it seems that Jesus is chastising Martha for choosing the lesser action, the tasks of hospitality and running a household versus listening attentively to him. Martha is distracted by many tasks, while Mary is quiet before the Lord. Jesus states that Mary has made the better choice for her time and energy.

Jesus' words must have been painful for Martha to hear, yet evidently she heard him clearly. When we later encounter the sisters in the Gospel of John, Lazarus has died and Mary is still sitting around the house. Martha, however, greets the Lord and engages in solemn conversation with him. She declares that Jesus is "the Messiah, the Son of God, the one coming into the world" (John 11:27). This is remarkable when you consider that the only other Jewish people to announce Jesus' true identity were John the Baptist and Simon Peter. Jesus told Peter that he knew the truth only by the revelation of God. I suspect that the same was true for Martha and John. Such revelations require us to "be still," that we might know God.

Rosalie sought to place God first in her life by prayerfully attending to God throughout the day. She offered specific prayers, prayed the Rosary (a series of prayers prayed by Roman Catholics), attended worship services, participated in a support group, read uplifting messages and stories about God's presence in the midst of our lives, relished life, and gratefully shared love with family and friends. Trying to keep God first takes effort, but, as Rosalie found, it brings the greatest reward.

Our own death or the death of someone we love is no more cataclysmic than the end of the world. By faith, the psalmist could see the end of the world and the establishment of God's peace, all the while trusting in God's presence and help. By faith may we also be still and perceive God's helpful presence in our midst.

Prayer Suggestion

In what ways are you aware of God's presence in your daily life? Be observant today or during the next week about where you see God and how you attend to God. We can experience God and turn our minds toward the divine in a multitude of ways. We can attend to God directly, through the world around us or through others. What ways are most natural for you? Remember, what works for one person may not work for another. For instance, different personalities prefer to pray in different ways. Commit to trying something new to center yourself in God each day. Consider focusing your thoughts on sunsets, the kindness of others, church, and so forth.

Prayer

O God, our Creator and Deliverer,
the whole world is in your hands.
You hold time, and you hold us.
Help us to stop and know that you are God.
Help us to find you in our midst and be filled with faith.
We need you, Lord. Help us to love you better. Amen.

WHY NOT ME?

For you, O God, have tested us;
you have tried us as silver is tried. . . .
we went through fire and through water;
yet you have brought us out to a spacious place.
Psalm 66:10, 12

As a child I learned that the American dream was a car, a family, and a home with a white picket fence. Today the nature of the dream has changed to financial prosperity coupled with the dreamer's unique interests and desires. The American dream has also changed in that people believe they are entitled to the dream's fulfillment simply because they live in America—not because of hard work or social position.

The same line of thinking causes us to exclaim, "Why me, Lord?" when something bad happens. We assume that our lives should go well, that we control our lives and thus are above disaster and tragedy. Bad things happen to other people. While we know (somewhere in our minds) that we are mortal, death is not real to most of us. Our reluctance to accept the reality of death is fueled by the delusion that medicine can heal everything. We expect science to have the power of God.

If we look at the realities of life and the complexity of human beings, it seems that a more reasonable question is, "Why *not* me, Lord?" We eat foods filled with chemicals and preservatives. Massive quantities of waste products fill our soil and air. Many of these wastes are toxic, including emissions from the cars we drive. Is it any wonder, then, that cancer is on the rise? We race around in high-speed vehicles and live in an age where the greatest poverty (among wealthy Western countries) is a poverty of soul and spirit. Our cities are full of desperate people. Bad things happen all the time to good people.

Psalm 66 refers to the oneness of God as the psalmist mentions the testings, burdens, and oppression God has allowed the people to suffer. Yet even in the midst of all this, the psalmist fans his hope in God by declaring God's steadfast love. Let's take a look.

PSALM 66:8-14, 16-20

Bless our God, O peoples,
    let the sound of his praise be heard,
who has kept us among the living,
    and has not let our feet slip.
For you, O God, have tested us;
    you have tried us as silver is tried.
You brought us into the net; you laid burdens on our backs;
    you let people ride over our heads;
we went through fire and through water;
    yet you have brought us out to a spacious place.

I will come into your house with burnt offerings;
I will pay you my vows, those that my lips uttered
    and my mouth promised when I was in trouble.

. . . .

Come and hear, all you who fear God,
    and I will tell what he has done for me.
I cried aloud to him, and he was extolled with my tongue.
If I had cherished iniquity in my heart,
    the Lord would not have listened.
But truly God has listened;
    he has given heed to the words of my prayer.
Blessed be God, because he has not rejected my prayer
    or removed his steadfast love from me.

Without a doubt, the most challenging issue that confronts the loving nature of God is the existence of evil and suffering. In seminary we talked about theodicy as a way of addressing this issue. Theodicy is a way to explain how a just and loving God can allow horror. Theodicy views evil in two ways: as moral evil or natural evil. Moral evil is what you and I normally associate with evil—the result of people choosing to disobey God. *Natural evil* is the term used for illness, death, and destruction through nature. Our concern is with natural evil.

Basically the dilemma for Christians and other religious people who believe in a loving God is this: How can a loving God allow us to suffer and die? The fundamental premise of theodicy is that God created a world in which we have choice. Evil is a necessary component in a world with free will.

Natural evil has been described as the shadow of life. In a picture the shadow accentuates the beauty and harmony of the whole. While we understand from the Bible that death is the result of Adam and Eve's sin, without death we would not change. If this life never ended, why would we aspire to grow or change? Through Christ we have been given eternal life, but our bodies are finite.

As the psalmist declares, this life is a testing time where we are tried just as silver is tried. It is a choosing time, whether to walk our paths our way or God's. We have burdens laid on our backs, and at times we have to travel through fire and water. God does not promise that adversity will not happen to us. The Loving One's promise is to be with us, sustaining and supporting us through life's difficulties.

I knew John was a remarkable person the first time I met him. Fifty years old, he had served as a chaplain in different capacities. His wife of twenty-five years and the mother of their children was dying of cancer. John's situation was particularly tough because his wife suffered the delusion that even her own family was trying to kill her, and she fought them when they tried to care for her. (Her change of personality resulted from her disease; nonetheless her family and hospice had to deal with it.) Finally she allowed one daughter to care for her considerable needs during the last weeks of her life. John tried to provide loving care to a sick and hostile wife while holding together a large family of parents, children, and grandchildren. He got exasperated at times, but he never complained. He never felt God had betrayed him or hurt him; rather, he was grateful for his wife, marriage, kids, hospice, and so on.

The incredible thing about John was that amidst living in his own hell, he constantly expressed genuine interest and concern for others. I was serving John at the time of my father's first stroke. John went out of his way to inquire about my dad and myself. His concern was heartwarming. We have all probably known people like John who, though their plates overflow with problems, are sincerely interested in others' well-being. Such people are a source of strength and inspiration for us.

Since we do not ask "Why me, Lord?" when good things happen to us, let us not ask "Why me, Lord?" when bad things happen. Let our attitude be "Why not me, Lord?" as we follow the psalmist's trust in God's loving presence with us. Let us hold to the promise that God is with us and for us.

PRAYER SUGGESTION

Spend time today reflecting on your situation. What are some of your blessings? What are some trials? Do you tend to ask, "Why me, Lord?" Ask God for the strength to endure adversities and the ability to overcome obstacles. Like the psalmist, believe and know that God listens to you.

PRAYER

Gracious and loving Lord, you are always with us, in the sunshine and in the rain, in sickness and in health.
Help us understand enough of the world you have created to realize that we have the choice to walk with you or without you.
Give us wisdom to accept your love and empowerment for our needs.
Let us be at peace, knowing that physical death is a part of life.

Let us be full of enthusiasm when life is good.
Let us be full of faith and trust when life is bad.
Give us the courage to face our own illness or to care
  for another's.
Grant us compassion and joy. Amen.

THANKFUL HOPE

We give thanks to you, O God;
we give thanks; your name is near.
People tell of your wondrous deeds.

Psalm 75:1

Terri was not remotely willing to give her husband up to death. You see, she loved him passionately. Passion is the only word that can really begin to capture their love and devotion. Terri was her husband's greatest joy and biggest cheerleader. She was totally committed to him and to helping him live fully as long as he could.

Letting go of her husband was hard for Terri. Once, midway in his journey toward death, she and I had a conversation about the gifts of life. We were talking about different provisions that had crossed their path. I tentatively commented, "All is gift." She resoundingly replied, "I'm not there yet." I certainly honored and respected Terri's position. Pain and loss can drown our thankfulness and our hope.

When I am able to objectively look at life, my only response can be, "I give thanks to you, Gracious One, for these marvelous gifts." Little blessings exist even in life's trials. I have osteoarthritis in most of my joints. I never thought I'd be able to live with nearly constant discomfort and pain, but I have discovered that I can. On days like today, I give thanks that I can take some pain pills and play golf on a gorgeous sixty-degree January day. Being outside in beautiful weather on the healing land is a gift. And thank goodness for the anti-inflammatory pills and pain pills that enable me to be able to play! The disease is a curse, the pills a blessing. I know that the psalmist who wrote Psalm 75 shares with me the experience of profound gratitude.

We are created for relationship. God never intended that we go through life alone but that we journey with God and others. Think about your faith over your lifetime. What has increased your faith? More than likely, the stories of others have been a significant factor in stimulating your faith. In fact, the Bible is a collection of such stories.

The Latin word *testis* is the root word for *testify* and *testicles*. When you testify, you reproduce the experience again. Hearing people testify about an experience with God triggers growth in our own faith. My friend Jerry's continual stories (he is the man I mentioned earlier whom God placed into my life at work) eventually moved me out of my state of unhappiness to the decision that I wanted the kind of faith he possessed, regardless of the cost.

Sharing stories is one of the many great powers in hospice work, especially when I am with families who are uncertain about an afterlife. I can share experiences that I and other hospice workers have had. Invariably the stories encourage them and increase their hopefulness. This truth, that stories have the power to encourage us, is one reason why I am writing this book and telling the stories of different people. God's name is near when we hear the faith stories of others. It reproduces in our life to increase our faith, which in turn increases God's power in our lives, which in turn leads us to thankfulness.

Often when we are in a depression or slump, it seems that we are all alone in the world. What a relief it can be to discover that we are not alone—that others have gone through or are going through what we are. There are many witnesses to faith. For instance, there is a continuity between the man who wrote this psalm, to all who have read it and been encouraged by it, to this moment when it speaks to you and me. These sacred words have given life and guidance to people for thousands of years.

During the nine months of Terri's husband's illness, she had to struggle with the reality of her husband's disease and any understanding of a loving God. Terri was raised in a Christian environment but did not consider herself a believer. By the time her husband died, she had formulated an understanding of death and God that helped her accept his death a little.

Four months later, just before Christmas, Terri and I had an amazing conversation. Terri remarked that she had no interest or enthusiasm for Christmas this year, which was certainly understandable. Then she described how, as she was walking into her house one day, the realization struck her that her beloved husband was in heaven celebrating Christmas with Jesus. His celebration this year was beyond anything we know on earth! This insight comforted her. Even though I have been a Christian practically all of my life, I don't recall ever having thought of Christmas from a heavenly perspective.

That week, as I met with several families whose loved one was going to die during the holiday, I shared Terri's insight. It was amazing how they, like me, had never thought of Christmas that way before. Thinking about Terri's realization somehow released some pressure and gave these families some perspective on their situations. Having someone die at Christmas is not quite so bad when you realize the loved one is with Jesus, celebrating in heaven.

Little in life is more powerful than our attitudes. A bad attitude can defeat us before we ever start anything. Similarly, a good attitude has the power to recreate itself. If we can be alert to our blessings and be thankful for them, we will begin to find more and more blessings to be thankful for. An attitude of gratitude brightens up everything in our daily lives. Taking the bad is easier when we know how much good exists.

The rest of Psalm 75 talks about God's judgment and the destruction of the wicked. What separates the psalmist from the wicked is his right standing with God and his attitude of gratefulness. He gives thanks to God and sings praises to God. Regardless of his circumstances, his power to give thanks and praise elevates him above his situation. So it is with us. A thankful heart breeds hope in our lives. Regardless of our circumstances, let us find something to give thanks for and sing praises to the One who loves us.

PRAYER SUGGESTION

Think about your situation. What have your sources of hope been? How have specific people or stories encouraged you? What stories can you tell to encourage hope in others? Today thank someone who has helped you, or tell a story to encourage someone else. Above all, give thanks to God for other people and for the hope we give one another.

PRAYER

*Precious Lord, illness, death, and exhaustion—they all
    bring us down, as though we are weighted with a heavy
    burden.*
Help us to hear stories of others that can encourage us.
*Help us to be a thankful people, filled with hope and
    courage for the future.*
*We thank you for those who have stimulated our faith by
    sharing their own faith. May we in turn lighten the
    load of others by sharing ways you have touched us.*
Help us to be a people with an attitude of gratitude.
You are our hope, thanks be to God. Amen.

An Undivided Heart

Teach me your way, O LORD, that I may walk in your truth;
give me an undivided heart to revere your name.

Psalm 86:11

Jin Young was twenty-two years old and full of uncertainty. I spent two and a half hours with her at her father's deathbed. He was dying from ALS (amyotrophic lateral sclerosis, or Lou Gehrig's disease), a horrible disease that destroys the body yet leaves the mind intact. Shortly after we got Jin Young's dad comfortable, she asked me to sit in a chair by the couch. She curled up in a quilt and began to talk.

Initially Jin Young talked about religion. Her father was a Roman Catholic and her mother a Protestant. She described each family member's religious beliefs and then revealed that she had considered herself a Christian until a year ago, when she had grown tired of the insincerity of Christians. She remarked, "It is hard to be a Christian."

Next Jin Young talked about her friends and what she was going to do with her life. She had one semester of college left before receiving her bachelor's degree. She asked whether I thought her best course of action was to finish college or to stay out a semester because of her grief. I asked her a series of probing questions to help her sort out her thoughts and feelings. After our discussion she asked her father if she should finish school this year, and he scratched out *Yes* with his pencil three different times.

During the course of our time together, Jin Young told story after story about her father's leaving Korea; his love for the United States; and his life, work, and happiness. She also relived numerous memories of her daddy from her growing-up years. Her memories took on a litany form, and I experienced a beautiful, sacred process. From what she said and what I witnessed of the man's spirit, clearly he was an exceptional person who knew the secrets of true life.

At the heart of her conversations about school, work, friends, and Dad were two themes: confusion about the important things in life and a desire to be everything good that her dad was. Her heart was divided about what to do and what values to embrace. The writer of Psalm 86 knew something about a divided heart, so he prayed for a whole heart.

PSALM 86

Incline your ear, O LORD, and answer me,
    for I am poor and needy.
Preserve my life, for I am devoted to you;
    save your servant who trusts in you.
You are my God; be gracious to me, O Lord,
    for to you do I cry all day long.
Gladden the soul of your servant,
    for to you, O Lord, I lift up my soul.
For you, O Lord, are good and forgiving,
    abounding in steadfast love to all who call on you.

Give ear, O LORD, to my prayer;
    listen to my cry of supplication.
In the day of my trouble I call on you,
    for you will answer me.
There is none like you among the gods, O Lord,
    nor are there any works like yours.
All the nations you have made shall come
        and bow down before you, O Lord,
        and shall glorify your name.
For you are great and do wondrous things;
    you alone are God.

Teach me your way, O Lord,
    that I may walk in your truth;
give me an undivided heart to revere your name.
I give thanks to you, O Lord my God, with my whole heart,
    and I will glorify your name forever.
For great is your steadfast love toward me;
    you have delivered my soul from the depths of Sheol.

O God, the insolent rise up against me;
    a band of ruffians seeks my life, and they do not set you
    before them.
But you, O Lord, are a God merciful and gracious,
    slow to anger and abounding in steadfast love
    and faithfulness.
Turn to me and be gracious to me;
    give your strength to your servant;
    save the child of your serving girl.
Show me a sign of your favor,
    so that those who hate me may see it and be put
    to shame, because you, Lord, have helped me and
    comforted me.

Discussing her confusion about priorities in life, Jin Young said that her friends were interested only in their money, clothes, and SUVs. She sensed somehow that these things were not important. Through her father's dying she was maturing from adolescence into a thoughtful adult.

I spoke with Jin Young about our fractured world and the power of simplicity. By simplicity I mean an intentional, inward focus on the most significant concerns in life. This inward attitude changes our outward nature as it becomes real within us. Christians focus on Christ and the kingdom of God. By centering on Christ, we center on his values. If I had to reduce these values to one word, *love* would be the word. If love guides our actions, then we will act in ways that affirm others. We will not lie, cheat, or hurt people. If we concentrate on being kingdom people, then the fads and pressures of the ever-changing world around us diminish.

Jin Young is very much a product of our culture. Her conversation revealed a scattered, fractured concept of the priorities in life. All of us are tempted to live in the surface world, primarily concerned with material possessions. However, because of her father's spiritual maturity, Jin Young knew somehow that the superficial path is not the way to live.

Our commercialized world tries to tell us how to spend our time, money, and energy. We become fractured and distracted and, consequently, do not live our lives as whole people, pursuing the important things in life. To survive as persons with values, integrity, and depth, we must learn to combat the voices of the dominant culture. Through faith we can struggle to remain centered in the most important values.

Another source of division can be the various roles we play, such as mother, wife, child, friend, and employee. Both illness and caregiving radically change our roles. In addition to being a daughter, Jin Young became an aide, nurse, and parent to her dad. Making this shift is challenging for anyone, but it is especially hard for young people to take on the role of caregiver for a parent.

How can we focus and relate who we are to the needs of those around us? By the power of our faith. Our faith can guide us to an undivided heart. First, prayer is a strong source of support, giving us the grace to do what we could not do on our own. Second, by stopping and being still, we will learn more about God and ourselves. Stillness of heart allows us to realize and understand the changes taking place around us and in us. Better understanding helps us to make the transitions. Will they be painful? Yes. Will they be successful? Hopefully.

Our psalmist recognizes that he is needy. He is also devoted to God and committed to his faith. He offers prayers and asks the Lord to teach him God's ways so that he may walk in truth with an undivided heart. The path of the psalmist is a guide for our own lives. We need to focus on God, who will enable us to become whole persons and to respond in hope and faith to the people and circumstances around us.

Prayer Suggestion

Take a "heart test" to find out whether you are whole or divided. How often do you feel shattered and fractured by the transforming roles you perform? Do you struggle to know what things in life matter the most? Set aside time in prayer to seek God's help and guidance.

God has a way, a path, for you to travel, and God desires to help you walk it. Awareness does not necessarily come instantly. You may need to reflect on these questions for a while; but as you learn more about yourself, you will be able to discern God's truth and walk in the Lord's way.

Prayer

Gracious Lord, help us to have undivided hearts.

Help us to live from the inside out, where our lives are guided by the weightier matters of love, hope, relationships, simplicity, and integrity.

You ask us to take on many roles, and sometimes these are downright hard for us. Give us, please, the strength and courage to become the people we need to be.

Give us the strength and courage to be unafraid of changes life asks of us.

Give us an undivided heart so that we might prosper as good people and give you the thanks and praise that you deserve. Amen.

HAVE MERCY UPON US

As the eyes of servants look to the hand of their master,
as the eyes of a maid to the hand of her mistress, so our eyes look
to the LORD our God, until he has mercy upon us.

Psalm 123:2

All of us need forgiveness; this need comes with the territory of life. For many of us life changes when we realize that God truly loves and treasures us as individuals. Fortunately our God is not content to merely create us and then to sit back and watch our lives unfold from a safe distance. No, the Creator is as close to us as our very breath, intimately concerned with and involved in our lives. I fully believe God weeps when we weep and rejoices when we rejoice appropriately.

Another life-changing experience occurs when we realize that God wants to forgive us for all of our wrongs. These wrongs include not just our social or private sins but also all of our shortcomings and moral failures committed against God, others, and ourselves. Forgiveness comes when we ask for God's mercy. We may still reap the consequences of what we have sown, but God does not hold our wrong choices and actions against us.

Forgiveness is also a healing part of most close relationships. I say this because we are human and imperfect, and so are our loved ones. At some point we or the ones we love will do things that require making amends and seeking or giving forgiveness. Failure to resolve misunderstandings erects barriers in our relationships.

Issues of forgiveness during illness come from two sources: events and actions before the illness and things that happen in relation to the illness. Stan is a good example of the latter. He was fifty-two when a hideous neurological brain disease struck him. Normal life expectancy for this disease is four months after diagnosis. The disease causes twitching, stiffness, and the eventual inability to communicate by speech or gestures. Stan's was a textbook case.

Perhaps the unexpected onset of such a debilitating disease at age fifty-two triggered Stan's anger. Or perhaps the frustration of being trapped in an excellently conditioned body sparked it. No one denied that he had a right to be angry. Unfortunately the nature of his disease prevented Stan's being able to process and defuse much of his anger in healthy ways. Regrettably, his wife became the outlet for his anger, which was painful for her to bear. After all, her husband, lover, and friend was dying, and she was forced to move from the role of wife and companion to being the caregiver for a bitter man.

In this situation Stan needed to ask his wife for forgiveness, and he needed to forgive himself. Even if Stan didn't ask for forgiveness for treating his wife unfairly, she still needed to forgive him—to release herself from the pain, anger, and hurt associated with his behavior. To heal the loss of her husband and to cope with his dying, she needed to seek the power of God's mercy for herself and let go of the bad feelings and memories. Through prayer she could ask God for the grace and mercy to forgive Stan.

An important thing to remember is that forgiveness does not make everything all right. What you did or what was done to you may be quite wrong. Though Stan was ill with a hideous disease, he had no right to mistreat his wife, who remained steadfast and lovingly by his side. Her forgiveness of Stan did not make what he did all right. Rather, her forgiveness untied her from the emotional burdens related to the wrong. When we forgive others, we release them and ourselves from the pain, hurt, and anger that we experienced. We no longer hold it against them.

What issues of forgiveness do you need to deal with? In what ways do you need to receive or extend forgiveness?

Psalm 123:1-3

To you I lift up my eyes,
> O you who are enthroned in the heavens!
As the eyes of servants
> look to the hand of their master,
as the eyes of a maid to the hand of her mistress,
so our eyes look to the Lord our God,
> until he has mercy upon us.
Have mercy upon us, O Lord,
> have mercy upon us.

Our psalmist has a good deal of humility. He knows his relationship with God—he is the servant, God the master; he is the maid, God the mistress. The word *humility* comes from the same root word as *humus,* or earth. To be humble is to be earthy, to know your place in the universe. When you're humble you don't think of yourself more highly or more lowly than you should. You understand your relationship to the world around you.

To seek mercy from God is to understand our wrongdoing and to ask God to cleanse us and renew us through forgiveness. When we are aware of sin or mistreatment against God or others, we feel a natural contrition or sorrow for what we have done. Accepting our imperfections and asking God for mercy frees us from the guilt, bad feelings, and negative emotions associated with our wrongs. We can even be released from the associated bad memories. To accept God's forgiveness, we must forgive ourselves.

Once we have experienced forgiveness, it is natural for us to extend forgiveness to others who have hurt us. They may not even know that we are hurt, but the powerful and healing results of forgiveness are still ours by our decision and actions to forgive. Sometimes we cannot communicate with the person we are forgiving. This does not need to prevent us from experiencing real forgiveness in our lives.

If we closely examine most of our relationships, we will find the need for forgiveness for others and for ourselves. We may even have to forgive God if the Holy One's plans do not match our own; it is part of our healing process with God. God does no wrong; but when God does not act in the way that we desire, we blame God, and that blame must be cleared away. And so it goes with our family, friends, acquaintances, and even enemies if we have them.

One of the most powerful and sacred moments I've witnessed involved forgiveness. Thelma had lapsed into a coma a day or so before I was called. It was time for her last Rosary. During the final stage of her illness, Thelma had moved in with her older daughter and her family. Her son also lived with them and helped care for his mother. Thelma's husband was working on a job site two and a half hours away and came home on the weekends. On this day all the family gathered around her bed, including the youngest, an estranged daughter from out of town.

The Rosary consists of five sets of prayers. Each of us led a set and offered a special prayer intention. While we were praying, all family members tearfully asked for forgiveness for anything they might have done that needed forgiving. Thelma's husband was careful to also ask God's forgiveness for his sins against his wife. The daughters requested forgiveness for specific actions. It was an emotionally powerful and holy time. When we finished, tears streamed from Thelma's closed eyes. On some level she had heard us and understood. Thelma's dying became a moment that empowered life—it brought healing and wholeness into the lives of her husband and children.

The experience was all the more powerful in light of the fact that Thelma had become mean during her last weeks of life. Much of the time she was not pleasant to be around because she was verbally cruel to her children. She did not act this way because she did not love them; it was a side effect of the poisons building up in her body from her renal failure. How miserable the family would have been if they had not sought forgiveness to clear up their past history or if they had allowed their pain from their mother's recent behavior to prevent them from forgiving her.

Why is forgiveness so important? Because it is the path to becoming a healed person. Even if we are physically dying, forgiving and being forgiven restore genuine life to us.

As you prepare for the future, take time to reflect on your life and actions. Be especially attentive to your present situation. If it is appropriate for you to ask for God's mercy, do so. If you need to ask for the mercy to forgive others, do so.

On a small piece of paper, write the sins others have committed against you. When you are ready to be released from these bad feelings and begin healing, burn the paper as a symbol of your forgiveness. Ask others to forgive you as appropriate. Experience the peace that comes from forgiveness.

PRAYER

Thank goodness you are a God who is slow to anger and abounding in mercy!

Have mercy on us, Lord, and forgive all of our wrongdoing.

Have mercy on us, Lord, and forgive all our sins against you.

Have mercy on us, Lord, and forgive all our sins against others.

Have mercy on us, Lord, and forgive all our sins against ourselves.

Give us merciful hearts and help us to forgive those who have sinned against us.

Help us to release our pains, hurts, and memories.

Bring us into your merciful peace and healing.

For we ask it in your name. Amen.

HELP, LORD, HELP

O God, do not be far from me:
O my God, make haste to help me!
Psalm 71:12

The older we get, the wiser we tend to become. The words of the wisdom writer in the Book of Ecclesiastes contain much truth: "For everything there is a season, / and a time for every matter under heaven: / a time to be born, and a time to die / . . . a time to weep, and a time to laugh; / a time to mourn, and a time to dance" (Eccles. 3:1-2, 4).

One of the beauties of Psalm 71 is that the psalmist speaks from the vantage point of old age and gray hair. God has been a part of the psalmist's life since conception. By examining the psalm, we can discover how a man who has depended on God throughout his life approaches the Lord in his later years.

PSALM 71:1-9, 12-22

In you, O LORD, I take refuge;
   let me never be put to shame.
In your righteousness deliver me and rescue me;
   incline your ear to me and save me.
Be to me a rock of refuge,
   a strong fortress, to save me,
   for you are my rock and my fortress.

Rescue me, O my God, from the hand of the wicked,
   from the grasp of the unjust and cruel.
For you, O Lord, are my hope,

my trust, O LORD, from my youth.
Upon you I have leaned from my birth;
    it was you who took me from my mother's womb.
My praise is continually of you.

I have been like a portent to many,
    but you are my strong refuge.
My mouth is filled with your praise,
    and with your glory all day long.
Do not cast me off in the time of old age;
    do not forsake me when my strength is spent.

. . . .

O God, do not be far from me;
    O my God, make haste to help me!
Let my accusers be put to shame and consumed;
    let those who seek to hurt me
    be covered with scorn and disgrace.
But I will hope continually,
    and will praise you yet more and more.
My mouth will tell of your righteous acts,
    of your deeds of salvation all day long,
    though their number is past my knowledge.
I will come praising the mighty deeds of the Lord GOD,
I will praise your righteousness, yours alone.

O God, from my youth you have taught me,
    and I still proclaim your wondrous deeds.
So even to old age and gray hairs, O God, do not
    forsake me, until I proclaim your might to all the
    generations to come.
Your power and your righteousness, O God, reach the
    high heavens.

> You who have done great things, O God, who is like you?
> You who have made me see many troubles and calamities
> > will revive me again;
> > from the depths of the earth you will bring me up again.
> You will increase my honor, and comfort me once again.
>
> I will also praise you with the harp for your faithfulness,
> > O my God;
> I will sing praises to you with the lyre, O Holy One
> > of Israel.

"Help, Lord, help!" is the psalmist's motto. The first thirteen verses are filled with supplications (prayers of request) to the Lord. In fact, the psalm alternates between supplications and affirmations of who God is. The psalmist says God is his rock, fortress, hope, and trust. He pleads with God, requesting that God never let him be put to shame, that God deliver and rescue him, and that the Almighty hear his prayer and save him. In spite of the psalmist's current situation, he proclaims that God has been his support since his birth, and he reminds the Creator that he continually praises God for saving him from many troubles.

The psalmist says that God has taught him since his youth. Two important lessons the psalmist learned are to praise God for God's wondrous deeds and to ask for God's help in all cases of trouble. In our key verse, the psalmist asks that the Provider who has sustained him from the womb once again revive him from the depths of the earth. Whether he literally means reviving from death to life, I do not know, but certainly as Christians we understand resurrection to be God's final saving act for each of us.

The diagnosis of a serious illness, especially in later life when it is age appropriate, can cause us to reevaluate our lives. This evaluation can lead us to doubt and question the path we have traveled. So it was with Dixie. She was a good woman who, by the world's standards, had lived a long life of relative ease. I am not suggesting that she did not undergo the trials that are a part of life. Dixie and her husband had endured one of the greatest tragedies parents can have. Their only son, a recovered alcoholic, died from cancer in his forties. Because it is not the natural progression of life for parents to bury children, recovering from such a loss can take a lifetime. Hopefully the parents recover from their grief, but often a reservoir of sadness remains just beneath the surface of their lives.

Dixie developed cancer in her late seventies. Though illness was age appropriate for her, she had not thought much about aging and death. Now cancer caused her to assess her life. Like many of us, in hindsight she saw that she had been the central concern in most of her decisions. She had been busy living life to suit herself, and she had not been terribly concerned about the needs of others. Dixie determined that she could have used her wealth in better ways, and now she felt remorse for having possessed so much wealth and using it so little to help others. As she faced her own death, she began to wonder how God might judge her stewardship of her life's resources.

Dixie had always been a Roman Catholic. Her faith had become much more meaningful to her and her husband when they had endured and survived all of their struggles with their son. As Dixie said to me, how could a parent endure the death of her only child without God's sustaining support? Clearly she and her husband intentionally grew spiritually during and following their son's illness and death. They turned to God and to the church for help during these challenging years. They moved beyond being pew warmers to become active, concerned members of their parish.

One of the primary ways God answers prayer is through other people. Our prayers of request to God can help us understand our needs. By putting needs into words we can evaluate their genuineness and make them more concrete. God's answers may surround us, but we must take the initiative to activate them. For instance, hospice is a wonderful work of God embodied in the flesh and blood of human beings. Hospice can provide terminally ill persons and their families with education, equipment, medicines, nursing care, home health aides, spiritual care, social work resources, and bereavement care. Hospice provides comfort care and companionship. I do not know a single person in our organization at Hospice Austin who does not have open arms and a caring heart for our patients and their families.

Dixie was willing to see me only every three weeks or so, but our visits always followed her agenda and lasted up to three hours at a time. We talked about everything from heaven and hell, to the nature of God and why the world is the way it is, to the death of her son and her concern for her spouse after her death. Hospice Austin provided an enormous amount of education to Dixie's husband. Having never cared for a dying person at home before, he relied heavily on their nurse for advice and direction.

Since their only son was dead, Hospice Austin played a vital role in the well-being of Dixie and her husband during the last months of her life. Throughout this time she and her spouse praised God and worshiped as they could. They lived out the psalmist's pattern of supplication and praise.

God, who weaved us together in our mother's wombs, will continue to love and support us through gray hair and old age on into death and resurrection. There is neither an age nor a place where we are outside of the Maker's faithful, loving care. As we remember that "for everything there is a season and a time for every matter under heaven," let us confidently stand in trust that all times are God's times. We will again be born; we will again laugh; we will again dance. Thanks be to God!

PRAYER SUGGESTION

Think of a time in your life when God rescued you from adversity. How was God's help manifested? Remember and give thanks. What are your needs now? In what ways have you asked God for help? How might God respond through the resources around you?

PRAYER

O God, our lives are not accidents but gifts of your love.
Remember us and care for us throughout our lives.
You have sustained us through our youth and given us
wisdom in old age.
We praise you and thank you for being our rock and
fortress, our hope and trust.

Though we face the unknown of death, revive us once more with your Spirit, that we might laugh and dance again in your heavenly kingdom. Amen.

A Cry for Help

The LORD is my strength and my shield;
in him my heart trusts;
so I am helped, and my heart exults,
and with my song I give thanks to him.
Psalm 28:7

When is it appropriate to cry for help? My mother was the type of person who didn't want to bother God about little things. I, on the other hand, sometimes consult God while grocery shopping (so that I will pick good, healthy foods)! I think it is always fitting to ask for God's presence and grace in time of need. It is good to be attentive to God in every situation and to lift up our concerns and those of others. When we need help we should ask for it, as it can deepen our relationship with God. We invite God into the midst of our situation simply by turning to God prayerfully.

What attitude do we need when we do cry out? For our prayer to be genuine, we must allow God the freedom to respond as God decides. We cannot prejudge God's response to our request because doing so turns God into a Santa Claus. The best attitude is one of expectant hope, remembering God's help in times past and anticipating that God hears us now and delights in comforting us.

Do you think that attitude makes a difference? Absolutely. People tend to die as they live. If you avoided life, that is probably how you will approach death. If you seized the marvelous gift of life, you will most likely approach death with peace and completeness. It is important to share our positive attitudes and hope with others.

PSALM 28:1-2, 6-9

To you, O LORD, I call;
   my rock, do not refuse to hear me,
for if you are silent to me,
   I shall be like those who go down to the Pit.
Hear the voice of my supplication,
   as I cry to you for help,
as I lift up my hands toward your most holy sanctuary.

. . . .

Blessed be the LORD, for he has heard the sound of
   my pleadings.
The LORD is my strength and my shield;
   in him my heart trusts;
so I am helped, and my heart exults,
   and with my song I give thanks to him.

The LORD is the strength of his people;
   he is the saving refuge of his anointed.
O save your people, and bless your heritage;
   be their shepherd, and carry them forever.

Without God where would we be? To the psalmist, God is life itself. If God does not respond, the psalmist says he will go down to the Pit—the grave—and will lose his life. The psalmist is helped simply by the act of trust. Isn't that interesting? His attitude is what matters when it comes to God's help. The psalmist is so confident in God's character that he is helped by simply knowing and having faith in God. His expectations are fulfilled. He then calls on God to save, bless, and guide his people.

At times our world falls apart, and we wonder if God is seeking to destroy us. We may believe that we are being punished for sins and shortcomings. Certainly we can be ill and experience catastrophes in our lives as the result of our own actions or choices. If you smoke, you may develop lung cancer; if you shoot up intravenous drugs with used needles, you may contract AIDS. These diseases follow the spiritual law of reaping and sowing. On the other hand, if with your lung cancer or AIDS you genuinely turn to God, it is the Beloved's compassionate nature to care for you.

Our psalmist calls upon God to do three things: to save his people, to bless them, and to be their shepherd who carries them forever. The call for God to save creation reminds us that we are God's people, saved and treasured. We are God's heritage in a special way, for of all of God's creations, only we humans can make moral choices. Only we are made in God's image.

To bless is to confer good on someone. There is great power in the tongue. With our speech we have the power of life or death—the power to bless or to curse. The content of our self-talk is critical to our mental and spiritual health and well-being. People with low self-esteem usually play negative tapes over and over in their heads, usually hurtful things that others have said to them. On the other hand, people whom others have blessed tend to play positive messages in their self-talk.

The image of shepherd is used in both the Hebrew Bible and the New Testament. A shepherd guides and leads his flock tenderly and lovingly. The sheep love and trust their shepherd. Jesus said he was the good shepherd because he laid down his life for his sheep. One of my favorite passages is John 10:10 where Jesus says, "The thief comes only to steal and kill and destroy. I came that they may have life, and have it abundantly." I absolutely believe this statement. God has created a world of choice where bad things do happen to good people; but if we open our lives to the Shepherd, he will lead us into abundant life.

Deanna was an inspiring person. Like the psalmist, she was a person of great faith. Turning to God and trusting in God's steadfast love, she was empowered to battle cancer for fourteen years. During this time she went into remission twice. Over the years of treatments she became close to a diverse group of other cancer patients who went to the same clinic or were involved in the same cancer support groups.

Deanna's faith led her to commit to praying for her friends daily. In the early morning she took her coffee out on her porch and spent time with God. There she sought the strength to endure her day and find joy in her blessings. Then she prayed that God would bring a healing touch to the lives of her friends. She never knew who would be healed and who would not; she just prayed for them all. Deanna actively served the Great Shepherd as her compassionate heart embraced and uplifted others. Her unconquerable spirit inspired everyone around her, including the clinic workers who also found their place in her daily prayers.

On May 14 Deanna's body died, but I remember the words of Paul:

> Listen, I will tell you a mystery! We will not all die, but we will all be changed. . . . For this perishable body must put on imperishability, and this mortal body must put on immortality. . . . Then the saying that is written will be fulfilled:
> "Death has been swallowed up in victory."
> "Where, O death, is your victory?"
> "Where, O death, is your sting?"
> . . . But thanks be to God, who gives us the victory through our Lord Jesus Christ. (1 Cor. 15:51, 53, 54-55, 57)

In the midst of her death, Deanna emerged victorious. Indeed death had been swallowed up in victory—victory in this life and in the next. Thanks be to God!

PRAYER SUGGESTION

Speaking words of blessing encourages and affirms others. Because blessing is a life-giving activity, it also encourages the one who blesses. Think for a moment: Who was the last person to say or write a word of blessing to you? How did it make you feel? Who was the last person you blessed? Doesn't it feel good to lift up someone else? Practice random acts of kindness and blessing. You'll feel great.

PRAYER

Gracious and Loving One, you always desire our good.
Help us entrust ourselves to you.
Enable us to experience our salvation and know that we
*   are loved beyond measure.*
Aid us in realizing your presence with us,
*   both when life is difficult and when life is glorious.*
You have saved us and you bless us! Carry us forward into
*   life, our Giver and Guide. Amen.*

Even though I walk through the
valley of the shadow of death,
I fear no evil. . . .
You prepare a table for me
in the presence of my enemies.

                        Psalm 23:4-5

PART THREE | # The Shepherd's Table Feeds Us

O Lord, How Long?

I am weary with my moaning;
every night I flood my bed with tears;
I drench my couch with my weeping.
My eyes waste away because of grief;
they grow weak because of all my foes.
                              Psalm 6:6-7

The time comes when it is all right to let go of life. For everything there is a season. As there was a time to be born, so there is a time to die. There is no shame in dying. People sometimes feel terribly guilty about being ill and dying. My dad is so ashamed of his feebleness; but as I told him, it certainly is not his fault, and we love him no less for it.

Three days after my dad's second stroke, he and I shared an open and honest conversation. Fortunately, after both of my dad's strokes, he regained considerable use of his affected side. Nonetheless, after this stroke, we talked about what a sad situation it was and how he felt grieved at being so afflicted. He didn't fear death; in fact, he told me that he hadn't really given death much thought, even at age eighty-eight. Furthermore, he confided, at this point he welcomed death.

All of us go through the cycles of aging. We may not realize that yet, but it is still true. And we will all die. That is certain. So why don't we die well? Each individual decides how to cope with dying. If we die from illness, to a large extent we determine how we die. We can finish this life by denying that death is happening, or we can face death by encountering it head-on. Doing the latter takes courage and support.

Our loving God yearns to hear our grief and support us through the process of dying. Psalm 6 graphically describes the side effects of grief as the psalmist painfully cries out to the Lord. Perhaps you will find that he also speaks for you.

Psalm 6

O Lord, do not rebuke me in your anger,
    or discipline me in your wrath.
Be gracious to me, O Lord, for I am languishing;
O Lord, heal me,
    for my bones are shaking with terror.
My soul also is struck with terror,
    while you, O Lord—how long?

Turn, O Lord, save my life;
    deliver me for the sake of your steadfast love.
For in death there is no remembrance of you;
    in Sheol who can give you praise?

I am weary with my moaning;
    every night I flood my bed with tears;
I drench my couch with my weeping.
My eyes waste away because of grief;
    they grow weak because of all my foes.

Depart from me, all you workers of evil,
    for the Lord has heard the sound of my weeping.
The Lord has heard my supplication;
    the Lord accepts my prayer.
All my enemies shall be ashamed and struck with terror;
    they shall turn back, and in a moment be put to shame.

I can hear the psalmist wailing, "Be gracious to me, O Lord, for I am languishing; / O Lord, heal me, / for my bones are shaking with terror. / My soul also is struck with terror, / while you, O Lord—how long?" (vv. 2-3). Facing death is frightening. How can we *not* be intimidated by something so different from anything we have ever encountered? Death is an unknown of the greatest magnitude! Terror can strike our hearts, but the Loving One is ready and willing to take that fear from our hearts and replace it with a sense of peace. Feeling peaceful about death may take some work, but all things are possible with God. Everyone can arrive at peace. Sometimes we do not know where or how we survive some situations, but our Provider carries us through and sustains us.

A dilemma that comes up for many people is the question of suicide. As a way to escape the natural process of life and death, is suicide valid? I cannot speak for every person in every situation, but from my own examination of the issue, suicide is not an option for me. I feel strongly that only our Creator has the right to take back life. We must accept the path that we are given. After all, it is partly of our own making.

I dread the thought of being feeble and dependent in some nursing home. Egad! I'd hate it! But if that happens, so be it. It will be the path given to me. Yes, I am important, but so is everyone else. My extended existence may benefit someone else or even me.

We can be at peace with how old age and death come to us. My mother was a brilliant woman who had master's degrees in physics, chemistry, and philosophy. She read Latin and French for pleasure, but dementia reduced her to being unable to read my birthday cards seven months before she died. One blessing was that my mother didn't seem to know what was happening to her, but I cried out on her behalf, "O Lord, how long?" And with great grace, my mother endured her path.

Our path is not always what we would choose. Sometimes caring for others exhausts us. Most mothers and many fathers know what it means to become drained by caregiving. Illness similarly drains us. Even as workers in the end-of-life care, hospice and other medical people have to deal with an overload of grief. Pouring our hearts out to God in spoken or written words is a good way to relieve part of that grief. Grief builds up in us like water behind a dam. When it gets too high, some of it must be released. Doing so opens the door for healing and sustaining power in our hearts. God is one of those with whom we need to talk and share.

When you come to this process of openly grieving before God, do so with faith. The psalmist declares, "The LORD has heard the sound of my weeping. / The LORD has heard my supplication; / the LORD accepts my prayer" (v. 9). The psalmist is confident that God is in this with him! He is not alone in his crisis. We too can be confident.

PRAYER SUGGESTION

Write your own version of Psalm 6. Use words and images that speak most to your heart. Pour out your fears and grief, and let the Beloved carry your burdens and bring you peace.

PRAYER

Loving One, be gracious to us, for we are frightened
    and confused.
What does it mean to be ill?
What does it mean to be dying?
How can we find strength for our caregiving demands?
We are weary from grief, and we grow weaker each day.
How long, O Lord? How long?
Come fill us with your strength. Empower us
    with your life!
Hear our prayer and bring us peace. Yes, bring us peace.
Amen.

SLEEP IN PEACEFUL ASSURANCE

I will both lie down and sleep in peace;
for you alone, O LORD, make me lie down in safety.
Psalm 4:8

Have you ever been afraid to go to sleep? I have. As a child, I was afraid of death because I didn't understand it. I was probably between five and seven years old when I attended my first graveside service in a mausoleum where our family crypts are located. My memory of this experience is pretty vague except that I remember standing there, looking up, and seeing how incredibly tall the marble walls were. They seemed enormous and cold.

Later, when I was a preteen, my dad was considering going into the funeral business. I was aghast. I announced that I would run away from home if he did so! I remember asking my dad, "Why in the world would you want to be in the funeral business?" (I am sure that I must have been contemplating my imagined horrors of embalming, etc.) He responded that the funeral business involved much more than that; the business was all about comforting people and helping them during a rough time.

Please understand, this was during the same time frame I announced that if my parents got a black car, I would not ride in it! Amazing how we change. Twenty-six years later I bought a black car with black interior. I have conducted numerous funerals and work as a hospice chaplain, offering end-of-life care and spiritual support to terminally ill people and their families and friends. I have come a long way in overcoming my fears of death.

I remember a few times during my teens and twenties when I could not fall asleep at night for fear that I would die and not wake up. That fear actually kept me awake until dawn. My mother told me something once that has always stayed with me. We were driving home from out of town when I began to ask her questions about death and her feelings about it. I brought up my fears of dying. I told her that I could not imagine what it would be like not to exist as me. It terrified me. She wisely said, "Take heart, Ann. If there isn't anything after death, you won't know it!" I thought long and hard about that, and eventually her answer worked!

My faith frees me from a lot of useless worry and fear—worry and fear over matters I can do nothing about. Just like everyone else, I am going to die someday. Nothing, absolutely nothing I do, will stop that. But if I am right and we do join the loving Giver of life, how absolutely awesome that will be! And if I am wrong and there is nothing after this life, I won't know it; and again, I am freed from a lot of hopeless worry and fear.

My faith is grounded in a loving God who empowers us to be filled with love and a sound mind. Whenever I am frightened, I call upon my Companion to aid and strengthen me. The cause of my fear does not matter; I find comfort and strength from calling on God. I am grateful that my parents taught me to say prayers at night when I went to bed. Almost always my thoughts turn to God before I go to sleep. This habit sets the tone for a restful sleep. As our psalmist also discovered, we can seek peaceful sleep from God.

PSALM 4:1, 3, 6-8

Answer me when I call, O God of my right!
You gave me room when I was in distress.
Be gracious to me, and hear my prayer.

. . . .

But know that the LORD has set apart the faithful for
    himself;
the Lord hears when I call to him.

. . . .

There are many who say,
    "O that we might see some good!

Let the light of your face shine on us, O LORD!"
You have put gladness in my heart
    more than when their grain and wine abound.

I will both lie down and sleep in peace;
    for you alone, O LORD, make me lie down in safety.

I worked at our inpatient facility, Christopher House, for several months on two different occasions. Both times I found my dreams deeply disturbed for the first two or three weeks after I arrived. My dreams were full of crises and dying people. The energy from my intense days fueled my dreams at night.

Processing is one of the most demanding problems for people who work in inpatient facilities because you have no "windshield time." Those workers who see home patients have a little time to process and debrief between visits while they drive from one home to another. In an inpatient facility, you often only have a few feet in which to process. My dreams mirrored my days in many ways; my sleep was definitely not peaceful. In fact, some days were more peaceful than their related nighttimes. After a few weeks, I settled into the intensity, in part because I developed different methods for dealing with the stress and by-products of the intensity. On particularly stressful days, I spent time in the evening relaxing with candlelight and soft music. I wrote or talked about the events in a way that allowed me to process my emotions without compromising my patients' confidentiality.

Part of the miracle of peace is that we experience it in the midst of turbulent times. That is one way that we can know that it is God's peace, when it defies the situations in which we find ourselves. It becomes the peace that passes understanding. When we are hit with the stress that illness or tension creates, God is truly the place for us to go for sleeping safety. We can do several things to encourage God's gladness in our hearts. One is to alter our environment. Frequently I surround myself with soft candlelight and listen to soothing music while I meditate.

I am blessed with a deep, strong, abiding faith in God's active goodwill on my behalf. I have peace about life because I know that God loves me and everyone else. Knowing this experientially and intellectually fills me with strength—all the strength I need to love and enjoy life while surviving its losses, disappointments, wounds, and doubts. God's love is very much revealed to me in Jesus' birth, death, and resurrection. The presence of the Creator and the gifts of the Holy Spirit empower me to exclaim, "I will both lie down and sleep in peace; for you alone, O LORD, make me lie down in safety." No matter what happens to me (or to you), we will be all right. Stand firm in your faith in God's goodness, and you will be sustained. Believe and ask God to help you with your unbelief.

PRAYER SUGGESTION

Even if you don't have problems sleeping at night, you probably know someone who does. On behalf of yourself or someone else, what could you do in your or their surroundings to promote relaxation? Candles, music, art, flowers, meditation, reading, prayer, fish-tank gazing, and incense have all aided me in calming my whole being and growing closer to peace. See if there is something you can do externally to help you relax on those days when you feel heaviness inside.

PRAYER

Jesus, you have revealed the Creator's loving presence
with us.
Help us all to realize deep down inside this wondrous love
that you have for each of us.
Free us from fear so that we may lie down in peace and
safety.
But most of all, just help us to know this love and pass it
on to others. Amen.

HOPE IN
THE DARKEST VALLEY

Consider and answer me, O LORD my God!
Give light to my eyes, or I will sleep the sleep of death.
Psalm 13:3

Many clouds and rainstorms occur in the valley of the shadow of death. When I first met Ruth, she was somewhat withdrawn into her world of lung cancer. She slept through my first few visits while her daughter enlightened me on their amazing family history. The daughter herself was undergoing chemotherapy for cancer. One of Ruth's sons had committed suicide; the other son was, thankfully, a recovering drug addict.

Within a month of Ruth's coming to Hospice Austin, her daughter was in intensive care. She spent five days on a respirator. They got these problems fixed, but in less than a month she was in the hospital for major surgery. Was it any wonder that Ruth cried out, "How long, O Lord? How long?"

PSALM 13

How long, O LORD? Will you forget me forever?
   How long will you hide your face from me?
How long must I bear pain in my soul,
   and have sorrow in my heart all day long?
How long shall my enemy be exalted over me?

Consider and answer me, O LORD my God!
Give light to my eyes, or I will sleep the sleep of death,

and my enemy will say, "I have prevailed";
    my foes will rejoice because I am shaken.

But I trusted in your steadfast love;
    my heart shall rejoice in your salvation.
I will sing to the LORD, because he has dealt bountifully
    with me.

Our psalmist has been crying out to the Lord for a long time. He wonders if God has forgotten him forever. He begs God to consider and answer him. He pleads, "Give light to my eyes, or I will sleep the sleep of death."

We can fear or experience the "sleep of death" in two ways. First, we can be numb to life and asleep to the wonders and miracles that surround us. When we sleep this kind of death, we move like zombies through life, existing and doing what we must.[1]

People stay in the comfort of sleepiness because it is both familiar and less demanding. But since sleepiness does not engage us with reality, it does not offer much genuine joy and wholeness. People who are asleep do not take the great risks necessary for authentic love or personal growth. The saddest part of this sleep is that the sleeper could be awake if he or she were willing to risk and grow.

The second sleep of death is literal death. The psalmist prays for rescue from death, but eventually death will overcome us all. Because of God's own laws, God cannot grant us our prayers to ultimately avoid physical death. But we are not left in darkness, in aloneness, in nonexistence, for we have been given life forever with God.

Hope is a necessary component of our faith. At one retreat I attended, a woman had some stones with words carved on them. We chose stones to get a focal word for that day. I drew the word *hope*. As I was reading about hope, the author referred to hope as the "warrior spirit" that fights against defeat. I love that image. When I need to stir up my hope, I envision my warrior spirit rising within me to conquer fears and defeat.

For Christians, hope in the promise of resurrection can carry us through the fear of dying. We fix our hope in a place where every tear is dried and every song is love. Heaven is a place of perfect wholeness and harmony, a place of shalom. There are worse things than death. Existence without quality of life or with great pain are examples of fates worse than death. When I think of being demented, an empty shell of myself, I much prefer the thought of being in the Almighty's presence, whole and complete as a person. If death is our enemy, we will prevail because of the gifts of life God gives us.

Over the next six months of Ruth's life, things were a little quieter, though it seemed that something was always happening. While Ruth was not particularly religious, she believed deeply in God's existence. She also expected an afterlife but hesitated to think that her destination depended upon accepting and believing in a few religious statements. Ruth definitely favored God's mercy over God's judgment. She feared the unknown of death and liked to read books written by people who claimed experiences with the spiritual world.

By God's graciousness, Ruth experienced her own special event shortly before her death. She came from a family of several children but had not been particularly close to her siblings. After her lung cancer diagnosis, she began corresponding with her previously estranged older sister. Most of their conversations were over the telephone; but a few weeks before Ruth's death, God orchestrated a small miracle for both of them.

Ruth was in Christopher House, our inpatient facility, with a pain crisis. Her sister, also suffering from terminal cancer, was near death. She too became a patient with Hospice Austin and actually came to Christopher House to die while Ruth was still there. Two days after she arrived, Ruth's sister appeared to Ruth in her room and assured Ruth that she did not need to fear death, that everything would be all right. After Ruth experienced talking with her sister, she called the nurse and found out that her sister had just died.

Words cannot express what this miraculous visitation meant to Ruth in terms of her peacefulness. She herself died within a few weeks, but after her sister's death she no longer feared her own. Ruth was convinced that God allowed her sister to visit her so that she would feel safe in the ultimate transition of death. The visit was a source of hope to Ruth and to all of Ruth's family with whom she shared the experience.

The valley of the shadow of death contains many clouds, but the presence of clouds does not necessarily mean storms. And even when storms do come, our God will give us shelter. Even death is not final. So let us be patient and have hope, for it is on the darkest nights that we look up and see the most spectacular stars.

PRAYER SUGGESTION

The psalmist asks God to give light to his eyes. How could you best profit from some of God's light? Take the time to search your heart for where you need light; then ask the Provider for the guidance you need.

PRAYER

Show us, O Giver, your path of life and healing.
Relax and restore us inside and out.
Give us the strength to be patient and endure our bad
*   times.*
Give us the light and guidance we need to see our path.
Consider us and answer us, O Lord, or else we will sleep
*   the sleep of death. Amen.*

THE IMPOSSIBLE
BECOMES POSSIBLE

The LORD sets the prisoners free;
the LORD opens the eyes of the blind.
Psalm 146:7-8

I am amazed at how many people's situations become impossible at least for a time. Donna was having an impossible time. Her husband was under hospice care for his terminal cancer. He was unsteady on his feet and had other side effects resulting from changes in his medications. Donna's health problems flared up, and she needed surgery. Her mother was in a nursing home some fifty-five miles away, and Donna carried the responsibility for her as well.

Donna needed someone to care for her husband, her mother, and herself for at least two months. Donna's brother, who lived out of town, was one possibility. But he too was facing surgery. Donna's impossible situation required an impossible solution's becoming possible, and that is the heart of our brief psalm verses today—God makes the impossible possible.

Since the beginning of time, God has been in the business of miracles. Perhaps you have experienced answered prayers that were wonderful surprises. Miracles certainly bring us great joy. It is wonderful when the impossible becomes possible.

After a week or two of problematic possibilities came a week of blessings for Donna and her family. The surgeon agreed to postpone Donna's surgery for three months so that she could care for her husband. Donna found an excellent nursing home only fifteen miles away for her mother and moved her there. Her mother's new doctor diagnosed an infection and began treatments that improved her condition. Donna's husband's CAT scan showed that some of his bone tumors were gone due to the treatments he was undergoing. It was all good news. The impossible situation became not only possible but also a blessing. In the midst of the painful desert came an oasis of blessings—a week full of rejoicing and laughter.

Later during her husband's final weeks of life, Donna's brother was able to come and provide comfort, space, and nurture for Donna to get some rest and pay some bills. Another impossible situation, standing by her spouse while he was dying, became possible for Donna through the loving help of family, friends, and hospice workers.

PSALM 146:7-8

The LORD sets the prisoners free;
the LORD opens the eyes of the blind.

One of the great blessings in working for Hospice Austin is being part of a secular organization that practices the love ethic of Jesus. Hospice Austin respects every person and offers everyone the same competent, compassionate services and care. About 5 percent of our patients are charity cases, but the hospice treats them no differently than paying patients. People who lived on the streets or in cars come to our inpatient facility to die. People who cannot afford medical insurance receive end-of-life care. I feel blessed to be part of an organization that helps all kinds of people during a most difficult time. God works through Hospice Austin to make the impossible become possible for many people.

Do you need the impossible done? If you turn to God, you have come to the right place. God may not answer your wants—like being cured or having as much time on earth as you desire, but God will give you what you need and more. It is helpful to remember that the goal of life is not an achievement or a destination. The goal of life is found in the process of living; it is being actively present in and for each season of your life.

Our knowledge is incomplete; God's is total. So if you need the impossible done, believe, trust, and have faith that God will provide. For "the LORD sets the prisoners free; / the LORD opens the eyes of the blind."

PRAYER SUGGESTION

When was the last time you had a need met unexpectedly or in a surprising way? Thank God for making impossible situations possible in your life. Are you inclined to dismiss God's provisions as coincidence? Believe in God's work among us, and pray specifically for the providential solutions to an impossible situation about which you are aware.

PRAYER

Lord, you are an awesome God.
You set the prisoners free and make the impossible possible
in our lives.
Our situations are never without hope because you have a
multitude of ways to reach us and help us.
Open our eyes that we may see your provision and give
thanks for it.
Open our eyes that we might see our salvation and
embrace it. Amen.

PROSPERITY IN OUR CIRCUMSTANCES

Happy are the people to whom such blessings fall;
happy are the people whose God is the LORD.
Psalm 144:15

It was my first call to visit a patient in the middle of the night. I dragged myself out of bed and dressed, all the while telling myself that I could wake up and drive the seventy miles to the patient's home and back.

I will always remember my visit that night to South Austin. The house was old, tiny, and full of people. The twelve-by-twelve-foot room must have held some thirty-five women, men, and children. I thought, *This man must have a dozen children!* But the dying man had only one child, a son who was present along with his pregnant wife and child.

I looked around the room. Who were all these people gathered at this man's deathbed? There were two women with young children sitting across from the patient's bed. A blonde Caucasian woman was in the corner near the bed. As I waited with this large family, one by one they shared their stories.

The ill man, Raule, and his family had immigrated to the United States from Cuba twenty-five years before. Raule's passion was helping people. The two young women were indeed related; they were sisters Raule had rescued, along with their parents, in the wee hours one Saturday morning twenty-two years ago. Their car had broken down; Raule stopped to help them and became a friend for life. They too were Cuban.

The blonde woman was a neighbor who had gone through a time of great hardship. Raule had been her friend and household repairman. Then there were the two brothers in their teens. They had no father in their lives when they met Raule, but he became for both of them the father they had always wanted and needed. As I looked around the home's meager surroundings, I was overwhelmed with the blessings of this man's life. How awesome that over the years, he had touched people's lives, and that once touched, they became friends for life. Raule's life was filled with the prosperity of faith, friendships, and family. His deathbed was holy ground for all of us.

PSALM 144:1-2, 3-7, 9, 12-15

Blessed be the LORD, my rock,
    who trains my hands for war, and my fingers for battle;
my rock and my fortress,
    my stronghold and my deliverer,
my shield, in whom I take refuge.

. . . .

O LORD, what are human beings that you regard them,
    or mortals that you think of them?
They are like a breath;
    their days are like a passing shadow.
Bow your heavens, O LORD, and come down;
    touch the mountains so that they smoke.
Make the lightning flash and scatter them;
    send out your arrows and rout them.
Stretch out your hand from on high;
    set me free and rescue me from the mighty waters,
    from the hand of aliens.
. . . .

I will sing a new song to you, O God.

. . . .

May our sons in their youth
    be like plants full grown,

> our daughters like corner pillars,
> > cut for the building of a palace.
> May our barns be filled, with produce of every kind;
> may our sheep increase by thousands, by tens of thousands
> > in our fields, and may our cattle be heavy with young.
> May there be no breach in the walls, no exile,
> > and no cry of distress in our streets.
> Happy are the people to whom such blessings fall;
> > happy are the people whose God is the LORD.

Though I knew Raule only in the passing moments of this life, I saw that he was a man of courage. A devout Roman Catholic, he recognized that relationships are the most meaningful part of life.

The psalmist speaks of God as one who trains our hands for war and our fingers for battle. Raule's warfare was his indomitable love that expressed itself in daily actions. His faith and his hope were weapons of prosperity in the face of death.

Raule was willing to help any person regardless of race, age, gender, or creed. He squarely faced and encountered life, people, and God. He was a warrior for God because he did not let dangers or hardships stop him from reaching out to help people in their time of need. We too can be brave in facing our future because the One who holds time holds us. If God is our rock, then our foundation is firm. We can trust, hope, and love. We can find meaning in our lives as well as the presence of the Giver and the gifts.

Illness can turn our lives upside down. It challenges and changes every aspect of life as it shatters our dreams. In the shadow of death, our situation can seem bleak and empty. To move out of that darkness, we need to look around and see our prosperity. After all, as the psalmist points out, God regards us! God thinks of us! Yes, you and me. The Divine One offers to be our rock, fortress, stronghold, deliverer, shield, and refuge. God provides for us in the midst of our illness.

Because of God's love for us, we can legitimately have an attitude! This attitude becomes our central means of overcoming depression, fear, and loss.

Through the lenses of our positive attitude, we can see our prosperity. To be able to do this, we must be aware of the Giver and the gifts of life. The greatest gift of all is the Giver. All things came into being through God, so, by definition, nothing is greater than God. How amazing it is that the Creator of the universe, the Giver of all, is mindful of us! God cares for each of us and actively seeks us out in loving relationship. To know that God loves us is an unparalleled experience in life. To truly appreciate the gifts of life, we must have some sense of God, our greatest Gift.

The other part of the secret to the psalmist's happiness is realizing the gifts of life one has and then treasuring them. For the psalmist these gifts include children, animals, produce, and safety. When the psalmist says, "Happy are the people whose God is the Lord," the psalmist recognizes God as the source of happiness from whom blessings come. This knowledge of God's provision, more than anything else, reveals one's life as possessing prosperity and abundance. John 10:10 records Jesus' teaching that the thief comes to steal, to kill, and to destroy, but Jesus comes not only to bring life but life abundant. Illness and death do rob us, but even in their reality, abundant life exists. We may have to search for it, but it is there.

Do you have people who love you? If you answer yes, then you are truly blessed, for to love and be loved is the greatest joy in life. Do you live in a home with indoor plumbing and electricity? Do you have food, water, and a car? Do you have a newspaper delivered to your home? Do you have family and friends who support you? Are medical treatments available to you? These are all gifts of prosperity for which we can give thanks.

As critical as all these gifts are to our well-being, the Giver is always the greatest gift. Our lives are not just for now, for this earth. Our lives with God are forever and ever. Our time on this earth is but a breath, a passing shadow. Let us call on God to be mighty in our circumstances. Because God is on our side, prosperity is ours. The Divine One is for us and with us and within us.

Therefore bless God; praise the holy name of the Lord of life. Sing a new song of joy and hope. God is with us!

Make a list of the blessings you enjoy. The psalmist mentions children, animals, produce, and safe communities as blessings. Reflect on your gifts and give thanks.

PRAYER

Almighty God and Giver of all gifts, you matter more than the gifts.

You are our rock and our fortress, our stronghold and our deliverer.

You give each of us bountiful gifts for ourselves and to share with others.

Be with us in this shadow of death. Scripture says that even darkness is as light to you.

Reveal to us some light and guide our attitudes.

Help us to count our blessings, for happy are the ones whose God is the Lord. Amen.

Today Just Relax

Your word is a lamp to my feet and a light to my path.

Psalm 119:105

Though I visited her only three times, being around Katy was one of the toughest things I've ever had to do. This small, wiry forty-six-year-old woman was a challenge at best. Her husband was dying of cancer. When I met them he was no longer able to eat; in fact, he was "preactive"—his body was beginning to shut down, and it would only be a week or two until his death.

As she sat and visited with me, Katy continually turned to her husband and yelled, "Honey, don't you give up. You hear me? You've gotta live. Don't you give up! You hear me? You're not going to die. Now, Baby, you gotta get better. Do you hear me? You gotta get better." He tried so hard to please her. He never raised his voice, but he softly pleaded with her to just let him go. She literally could not bear the thought of his death, of his absence from her. Her habit of yelling at him was unnerving and stressful.

The third time I was with them was extraordinarily hard. It was almost 5:00 P.M., Friday, December 10. I'd had an exhausting day. I knew our visit would be unsettling, and I just wanted to go home. But when I had visited Katy and her husband on Monday, I'd told them I would return on Friday. As much as I did not want to go, I had the feeling that I needed to. So I went.

As soon as I arrived at their apartment, I knew that something was wrong. Through the door, I heard Katy wailing. Knocking and calling out, I braced myself as I stepped inside. I walked back to the bedroom, and there they were. He was dead, and she was beside herself with grief. She straddled his chest, screaming at him, "Breathe, Baby, breathe. O God, O Jesus, don't take him! Oh, Baby, come back!" For one and a half hours I held her while she wailed and screamed.

The downstairs neighbor called 911. Fighting the rush-hour traffic, the police, fire department, and ambulance all arrived about thirty-five minutes later. I explained to them that the man was a Hospice Austin patient with advanced liver cancer who had been dead for at least thirty-five minutes. But since the patient did not have a "Do Not Resuscitate" order, the emergency teams were legally bound to try to revive him if the wife wished it. She did. I held her and comforted her as best I could with pats and reassuring words. Meanwhile, to my horror, they worked to revive the broken body. Mercifully, they were unable to revive him. Katy remained inconsolable in her grief. After I had been there for one and a half hours, Katy's mother and sister arrived to help her, so I excused myself and went home.

I was in a state of shell shock when I exited Katy's apartment. I called the hospice team and left a voice mail message, then drove the thirty miles home, wondering what in the world I was going to do to alter my emotional state. You cannot go through an intense experience like this and then just come home and have a normal evening with family or friends.

As if God were preparing a place for me to heal, shortly after I arrived home, everyone else left to do one thing or another, which gave me space and peace. I was drawn to find some music but not the music I normally listen to. I found a CD sampler and put it on. The music was stirring and beautiful. Moving by some gut instinct, I got out my *Art for Little Texans*, a wonderful coloring book for children of all ages that has pictures by different Texas artists. I found a drawing of the backs of two Indian women. Entitled "Shoulders with Me," the picture shows one woman resting her head on the other woman's shoulder. Seeing this picture as symbolic of my relationship with Katy, I spent the next hour listening to the wonderful music and coloring the picture. As I colored, I offered prayers for Katy's healing and for my own. The timing was perfect, because as I finished the picture, the first family member arrived back home. During the hour that everyone was gone, I experienced a deep healing for the wounds I had received that afternoon. My whole being had been restored—body, soul, and spirit.

PSALM 119:105

Your word is a lamp to my feet and a light to my path.

Do you ever feel like you're walking almost entirely by faith? I do. God's "word," alive and glowing, guides me and gives me inspiration. As I found out later, Katy had asked our social worker to cancel my appointment for that afternoon. I had not received the message, and I have no doubt that God ordained my timely arrival. Through God's word the Almighty communicates with us, instructs us, and guides us. This word can be embodied in many different forms besides the written word, such as the promptings of the Holy Spirit or other people, nature, art, or music. In this significant healing event for me, God's word, God's light and lamp to my path, took the form of promptings, music, and art.

In my work, I experience God's healing, relaxing word embodied in many ways. The most common way, of course, is in the written word. The psalms we are reading are God's written word; they fit the realities of our situations and offer us hope and encouragement. In addition to the scriptures, thousands of uplifting books bring God's word, fresh and revealing. I frequently find devotional books and Bibles in easily accessible places in my patients' homes.

God's word is also embodied in creation. Having always felt connected to nature, I spend as much time as I can outdoors. When I visit my elderly dad in Oklahoma City, I find my walks to be an integral part of my healing process. This is especially true when I walk at Lake Hefner with its abundant wildlife; I am conscious of all the life around me. Similarly, I notice nature when I drive to see my out-of-town patients and take back roads rather than interstates and major highways. Driving the back roads is relaxing and healing as I observe the seasons of the year and watch the crops of hay, corn, maize, and cotton from planting to harvesting. I am reminded that death and life are part of the same mystery. They are common to all living things. God's word in creation can be a healing word.

God's word can also be enfleshed in art. Viewing an art show can help us escape our present situation and at the same time increase our peace with the mystery of life and death as we see other places and people through the artist's eyes. Doing art, as I did in this case, can be healing. Several of my patients do art as a creative expression of their spirituality.

Art also offers other benefits. Chuck didn't want to spend his last months in front of a television. Instead, he took up painting by number. Until a couple of days before he died, he and his wife painted whenever he had the strength. With great determination he finished a dolphin painting right before he died. His youngest daughter, who was so present and helpful during his illness, now proudly displays it in her home. The painting was a special gift of love.

God's word can also come to us as music when it reaches way down into our souls, healing us. Music is a universal language that shapes and molds our emotions. I frequently use music when meditating.

Experiencing God's word as a lamp unto our feet and a light unto our paths requires us to be open and discerning to the world around us and within us. When we are relaxed, we have more energy to listen and perceive. The world around us can be a source of God's guiding illumination and healing ways. We must also look within ourselves for the presence and leading of the Holy Spirit. God will light our path for us, perhaps only a step at a time. But God will provide light for regular processing and healing, as well as for all of the decisions of our life.

PRAYER SUGGESTION

Relaxation is a key to being open to hear or experience God's word around and within us. Find a calm activity you enjoy. It can be walking, painting, dancing, singing, gardening, or any other activity that relaxes you as you are absorbed in it. When you feel the need to relax and be refreshed or healed, do your activity. Allow yourself to become absorbed in doing it. Be relaxed and reflective. Let your actions become a reflective meditation on God's light and presence with you. Relinquish yourself to your task and to God.

PRAYER

O Guider of the path, shine light before us to guide us in
your ways.
Be a pillar of fire before us to safely carry us into the
future.
Be an inward light to warm our hearts and nudge us in
your way.
Guide us from within and from without.
Show us your path of life and healing.
Relax and restore us inside and out. Amen.

THE HEALING POWER
OF GRIEF

Weeping may linger for the night,
but joy comes with the morning.
Psalm 30:5

The title of this devotion may seem strange. Isn't grief a negative process? Yes and no. Grief is an intense, emotional suffering due to loss. We experience loss when we change jobs or move, when we lose friends or give up bad habits, when our hair falls out or we turn forty. Illness and caregiving certainly place us in situations of loss and therefore grief. In reality, we experience grief on some level whenever we have a loss. Change, loss, and grief all seem to go hand in hand. They are also an ordinary part of every life.

While grief is a painful process, our response to it can produce growth and healing in our lives. Certainly such achievement is costly, but we are better off having something good to show for our pain than nothing at all. When we are able to gain from the destructive, painful circumstances in life, then we can say that they are in part redeemed. The Bible is full of stories of hardship and tragedy that end up bearing blessings. Paul expressed it beautifully in Romans 8:28: "All things work together for good for those who love God." No story of redemption is greater than the Good Friday/Easter Sunday one.

All of us will experience grief many times. Though a painful process, grief can also help us become more mature and integrated. Working through grief can bring healing power to our devastated lives.

Psalm 30

I will extol you, O Lord, for you have drawn me up,
    and did not let my foes rejoice over me.
O Lord my God, I cried to you for help,
    and you have healed me.
O Lord, you brought up my soul from Sheol,
    restored me to life from among those gone down to
    the Pit.

Sing praises to the Lord, O you his faithful ones,
    and give thanks to his holy name.
For his anger is but for a moment;
    his favor is for a lifetime.
Weeping may linger for the night,
    but joy comes with the morning.

As for me, I said in my prosperity,
    "I shall never be moved."
By your favor, O Lord,
    you had established me as a strong mountain;
you hid your face; I was dismayed.

To you, O Lord, I cried,
    and to the Lord I made supplication:
"What profit is there in my death,
    if I go down to the Pit?
Will the dust praise you?
    Will it tell of your faithfulness?
Hear, O Lord, and be gracious to me!
    O Lord, be my helper!"

> You have turned my mourning into dancing;
>> you have taken off my sackcloth and clothed me with
>>> joy,
> so that my soul may praise you
>> and not be silent.
> O LORD my God, I will give thanks to you forever.

The psalmist declares, "As for me, I said in my prosperity, / 'I shall never be moved.'" At times we get carried away and begin to think that all of the good that happens in our lives results from our efforts. I do not mean to diminish what we do, but we accomplish nothing on our own. God provided our gifts of nature and nurture; we had little to do with them. God's timing led to my working for Hospice Austin and later opened a door for this book and birthed it in me. In our prosperity, we frequently forget the invisible hands beneath us supporting us.

It shocks us to realize we are not the ones in control of our lives! We lose our illusion of control, and this births grief in us. Like everyone before us, we too must leave this earth. No amount of desire or money can change that fact. We will lose our lives, and people we love will lose theirs. The grief process can heal us by bringing integration and wholeness to our lives. To work through our grief is to encounter it and win freedom from it. The psalmist credits the Lord with healing him and restoring his life. Losing a loved one or losing our own health drives us to the Pit. But with God's grace, our hard work, and time, we can receive healing.

Grief involves a number of stages, including shock, denial, and anger. These are perfectly natural responses when we have been let down. Illness presents the sick person with physical failure. In shock the ill one wonders, *How could my body let me down? Why didn't it let me know?* The caregiver thinks, *I can't believe my sixty-year-old husband is ill. What happened to our retirement years?* Understandably, shock is normally the first response to change and loss.

After shock begins to wear off, we frequently feel denial: *This can't really be happening. Surely this is a nightmare we will wake up from.* When we get to a point where denial is no longer possible or we are ready to move on, we may well become angry. Anger, frequently viewed as a bad emotion, can also be both healthy and natural. Anger is healthy when it is the response to the denial of a legitimate need. Since death is a natural part of every person's life, our anger eventually has to deal with that reality. As we begin to accept the reality of loss, we may try to bargain with God to save our loved one or to cure us of our disease. When that fails, we may lapse back into anger, but hopefully we will move to a place of peace or acceptance. Throughout this process depression and sadness may plague us.

Time is the greatest healer. As time wears on, we tend to look at our experience with greater reflection. We learn a great deal and can pass on our knowledge to others. We have lost, but what have we gained in place of the loss? Even with its negative effects, grief still can produce good in our lives.

As I write this meditation, I am returning home from a trip to Los Angeles with my friend Terri. We went there, along with an Austin filmmaker and his wife, to see his documentary film in the AngelCiti Film Festival. The documentary included the story of Terri and her husband. Our trip was especially meaningful for Terri because of several synchronized circumstances. First, the film's debut was Valentine's Day, a significant day for Terri and her husband. Last year they had spent it in a highly televised hot-air balloon ride. Second, the debut occurred exactly six months after his death. Additionally, we got excellent airfares and had a wonderfully nurturing stay with my cousin and his wife. Terri was able to spend the evening with an old friend she had not seen for years. We walked along the beach, and our spirits were uplifted by the beauty of the land and the J. Paul Getty Museum. The trip was a healing experience for Terri and me.

But Terri's grief is still painful. She will need several years to process the traumatic loss of the love of her life. She and her husband were married for less than a year, and she is working hard to survive her grief. Hopefully a time will come when she will complete the grief process. Certainly next year's Valentine's Day will be eased by remembering this one.

I want to make a distinction between grief and sadness. Grief is tied to specific events, and each source of grief can be worked through and completed.

In contrast, sadness can be a cumulative emotion. We can process our grief and get over it, yet still have a significant amount of sadness for the loss. For instance, my friend Terri will always be sad that her husband died so young, leaving her no children and turning their dreams to ashes. Yet the paralysis and depression caused by his death will fade.

Actively processing her grief is bringing healing change. Terri is still devastated. She is still in sackcloth and ashes, but a day will come when the grief clothes come off and her mourning will turn to dancing. Her confidence will be restored, and she will again be open to life. Will she always miss the love of her life? Absolutely. Will she always have sadness about his premature death? Sure. But she will also have the joy of embracing life again, not as a wounded person, but with a willingness to again risk loving. When she emerges on the other side of grief, she will know infinitely more about herself, life, and God than she ever did before. She will be more integrated and whole. This costly change is the healing power of grief. Thanks be to God that good can be redeemed from great suffering.

PRAYER SUGGESTION

Find a time and place where you will not be interrupted for an hour. Relax and get comfortable. Think about your grief and sadness.

What are some losses you have experienced? Write them down. In what areas do you have unprocessed grief? What losses have produced sadness in you? In what areas do you feel anger?

Spend as much time as you need to get in touch with the losses of your life. Then give God thanks for your life and ask for the strength to work through the grief, release the anger, and endure the sadness.

PRAYER

O God of life and death, sorrow and joy,
We come to you in sackcloth and ashes, devastated by
*   our losses.*
Hear us and help us.

Turn our mourning into dancing.
Remove the pain of our hearts and make them whole
  again, to your glory and our joy. Amen.

Nature Can Inspire Us

Those who live at earth's farthest bounds
are awed by your signs;
you make the gateways of the morning and the evening
shout for joy.

Psalm 65:8

I can't imagine life without the beauty of nature. God created us in the midst of the web of life and intricately wove us together with the rest of creation. Because we are connected to and interdependent with nature, the natural world can be a source of strength and life for us. I think I have known all my life that the land and the creatures that inhabit it are a powerful source of healing. As a young child, my greatest joy came from our frequent adventures in the country.

One of the most amazing nature experiences happened to my patient Katherine. She was fifty-one when she came to live at Christopher House. She made the move slowly and reluctantly. Katherine had a wonderful home out in the country that greatly nurtured her, and she hated to leave it. The only reason she did so was because she did not want to burden her sons anymore. She needed to be some place where she could be cared for, especially if she began having seizures caused by her brain tumors.

Katherine and her husband had built their dream home together. He had later become ill with cancer and died at home about three years before. Around the time her husband was diagnosed, he and Katherine had planted Indian butterfly plants all along their backyard. That summer their yard was ablaze with monarch butterflies. As time progressed, young caterpillars eventually wove cocoons all the way across the back porch of their home. During the final weeks of her husband's life, they watched daily the butterflies emerge

146

from their cocoons. On the day of his death, Katherine watched the last two shells yield their butterflies.

How beautifully nature mirrored her husband's transformation! They felt deep within their souls that God, the Creator of all life, was present with them in the blessing of the monarchs. This knowledge was a source of great strength and consolation as Katherine's husband was dying. We have to live through some pretty horrible situations. How wonderful that nature can be a healing strength for us.

PSALM 65

Praise is due to you,
    O God, in Zion;
and to you shall vows be performed,
    O you who answer prayer!
To you all flesh shall come.
When deeds of iniquity overwhelm us,
    you forgive our transgressions.
Happy are those whom you choose
    and bring near to live in your courts.
We shall be satisfied with the goodness of your house,
    your holy temple.

By awesome deeds you answer us with deliverance,
    O God of our salvation;
you are the hope of all the ends of the earth
    and of the farthest seas.
By your strength you established the mountains;
    you are girded with might.
You silence the roaring of the seas, the roaring of their
    waves,
    the tumult of the peoples.
Those who live at earth's farthest bounds
    are awed by your signs;

you make the gateways of the morning and the evening
     shout for joy.

You visit the earth and water it,
     you greatly enrich it;
the river of God is full of water;
     you provide the people with grain,
     for so you have prepared it.
You water its furrows abundantly,
     settling its ridges, softening it with showers,
     and blessing its growth.

You crown the year with your bounty;
     your wagon tracks overflow with richness.
The pastures of the wilderness overflow,
     the hills gird themselves with joy,
     the meadows clothe themselves with flocks,
     the valleys deck themselves with grain,
     they shout and sing together for joy.

In my opinion, nothing in the universe surpasses the beauty of a spectacular sunrise or sunset. The Creator's paintings at the start and end of each day serve as harbingers of hope, for with each new day comes the possibility of new beginnings.

Truly the universe inspires awe. When we are aware of the world around us, we realize what a small part of it we are. Whether watching the path of the moon or gazing into the nighttime skies, we are reminded of the incredibleness and giftedness of life. With God all things are possible.

The seasons of the year are another favorite way for many people to mark the passage of time. The changes in the natural world around us parallel the cycles of all life. Religious people who observe the holy seasons of the year know the power of following a sacred path of awareness each year. Experiencing winter, spring, summer, and fall in our own lives and relationships can also give us a path of self-awareness and self-examination.

Animals are another source of wonder. Sometimes pets can be rather interesting creatures. When I first visited Kent's house, I couldn't help but notice the pig art everywhere. I asked if he had a fascination with pigs, and his wife said, "Absolutely." For some reason Kent had always loved pigs. At this time in the progression of his illness, Kent could speak only a few words at best. His ALS imprisoned him. I asked his wife if she thought he would like a pig visit, and she thought it was a grand idea.

Hospice Austin is blessed with a tremendous volunteer force. I contacted one of our volunteer coordinators, who got busy immediately. Arranging for a pig to come visit turned out to be much more complicated than expected. It seems that pigs cannot climb stairs. Also, no matter how well trained they are, when they go into someone else's home, they can go wild from sensory overload.

Since Kent's front porch had stairs, and his house was crowded, we decided to look for alternative ways to unite Kent with a pig. Through the volunteer network we finally discovered a couple who had rescued some thirty-five pigs. They literally had a pig mansion in the pine forest near Smithville. We set a date for a field trip to visit the pigs. It just so happened that Kent's mother and son were visiting from Colorado, so the five of us went together. Kent had a blast. The owners let the pigs out one at a time to come visit Kent. He gave them peanut butter cookies, which they loved. We also met several litters of piglets. The couple explained a great deal about pigs' physical and psychological behavior.

All I have to do is close my eyes and I can see us all there—Kent grinning from ear to ear as we heard each pig's story and he gave them a cookie. The adventure fulfilled one of Kent's desires and gave everyone else a welcome respite from the everyday routine of illness.

Nature can indeed inspire us and give us much pleasure. Take advantage of our connectedness with nature, and let the natural world around you strengthen your spirit.

What in the natural world lightens your heart and gives you pleasure? How does the current season of the year mirror what is going on in your life? Perhaps your pets bring you great comfort. Whatever strengthens you, be attentive to it as God's gift to you and give thanks for it.

PRAYER

God of heaven and earth,
You are the Maker of the lands and the seas.
Help us to appreciate the loving works of your hands.
Help us to realize the value of all life.
Help us to accept your everlasting love for each of us.
Open our eyes to see the healing wonder of nature
    around us.
Open our hearts to receive nature's gifts.
May nature always enhance our lives. Amen.

GOD STICKS WITH US

Know that the LORD is God.
It is he that made us, and we are his;
we are his people, and the sheep of his pasture. . . .

For the LORD is good; his steadfast love endures forever,
and his faithfulness to all generations.

Psalm 100:3, 5

The way we view God is fundamental to our happiness in life. Is God one who loves us and is with us and for us? Or is God the enemy who wants to rob us of the gift of life, one who delights in our trials, or perhaps worse, one who couldn't care less what happens to us? If we can dare to trust and believe in God's love for us, we will be open to experiencing God's provision in our circumstances. We will feel the presence of an indescribable strength in our lives. We will know a source that empowers us to do what we could not do on our own. We will be sustained in the midst of great adversities.

Vincent loved his wife deeply. She had always handled all of the indoor chores while he financially supported them. Even though they had three children, he had never changed a single diaper. Then his wife became ill with cancer at age forty-two. At fifty-five she became bedfast. Vincent began to express his love for his wife by doing everything that she had previously done, including changing her diapers and caring for her personal needs. He did not know a great deal about the God talked about in churches, but he knew a great deal about the Giver of life. By God's power from deep within himself, Vincent found the ability to do tasks he never thought he should or could do. God's grace enabled him to love his wife fully and sacrificially.

At times all of us experience the feeling that God is absent from our lives.

151

In reality, though, I believe that God is always present with us. When we feel like God is absent, perhaps it's because God has some reason for not revealing presence just then. But the primary reason we have trouble discerning our Creator's presence, I believe, is because we don't still ourselves long enough to look and listen.

This truth is illustrated in the story of a father who took his daughter into the woods for a walk. The father was trying to find a path through the woods. He saw a ledge ahead and told his daughter to stay put while he went to look out and determine which way they would go.

Shortly after he left her, three butterflies came breezing by. Enraptured with them, the young girl danced off behind them. When they finally floated away from her, she realized that she was lost. She ran here and there, crying out all the while, "Daddy, Daddy where are you?" She tried to find the place where she had been with her dad, but she was hopelessly lost. Finally, exhausted and frightened, she plopped down on the ground, leaned up against a tree, and cried herself to sleep.

Soon she awakened to her father's presence. "Daddy, why didn't you come find me?" the daughter cried, feeling miffed and hurt. Her dad responded, "Honey, when I was on the ledge, I saw you chasing the butterflies. I knew if I came down from the ledge I would lose you in the woods. So I have been on the ledge all this time, watching you and waiting for you to settle down so I could come to you." This analogy is true for each of us at times. God can't reach us because we don't make ourselves available to God. We have to stop, sit down, and lean against a tree so that God can approach us.

We get lost in illness and death. They disrupt our normal lives and bring trials we do not want. Time and time again, people are sustained by their faith. Because God loves each of us with a steadfast and everlasting love, God carries us through hard times. Truly, even in our hardships we can find things to be thankful for.

Psalm 100

Make a joyful noise to the LORD,
    all the earth.
Worship the LORD with gladness;
    come into his presence with singing.

Know that the LORD is God.
    It is he that made us, and we are his;
    we are his people, and the sheep of his pasture.

Enter his gates with thanksgiving,
    and his courts with praise.
Give thanks to him, bless his name.

For the LORD is good;
    his steadfast love endures forever,
    and his faithfulness to all generations.

Since I was a city girl, I did not know a great deal about sheep and shepherds. A British teacher came as a guest speaker to the church I attended and spoke on shepherding during biblical times. I learned that shepherds and their sheep had a close relationship. Shepherds were known for their love and steadfast faithfulness to their flock. They defended their sheep with their bare hands if they needed to in order to keep them safe from wolves, bears, and any other threats.

Sheep, it seems, were relatively dumb animals. They required the guidance of a shepherd to have abundant food and water. While some wayward lambs managed to break a leg on their own, other willful lambs had to have a leg broken so they could be tamed and saved from their own stupid behavior. The choice was either to break the willful lamb's leg or let the lamb get itself killed. In both cases, the shepherd would bind the injury and carry the animal on his shoulders until it could walk on its own. During this time, the shepherd and lamb would bond and the lamb came to know, love, and follow the shepherd's voice.

I find it humbling to think of myself as a sheep. When the psalmist makes the joyful sounds of Psalm 100, he knows what it is to imagine God as the Great Shepherd who has made us, for "We are his; / we are his people, and the sheep of his pasture."

God's will is a complex subject. Certainly God's perfect will for our lives differs from God's will in the circumstances of our lives.[1] In other words, God does not want us to have broken legs or broken bodies because God gets some sort of pleasure out of our suffering. God's perfect will for us is that we become fully the people we were created to be, in God's own image. God wills that we become whole and complete—that we be filled with love, joy, and inner peace and that we live in harmony with the universe that surrounds us. This is God's perfect plan, our future in the life to come.

But God has chosen to create a world in which death is a part of living, a world in which we have the free will (within the confines of our life circumstances) to make our own choices and to choose our own path—with or without God. Natural evils can befall us, like tornadoes and illnesses, and moral evils are born of bad choices. The world is created as it is so that we can strive and choose to be good people in God's image. Can there be joy without sadness to define it? Can there be right choices without the freedom of bad choices? Within this world of good and evil, God has a circumstantial will—or a will for our circumstances. Included in this circumstantial will is that we all die.

Some of us die by accident, by the choices we or others have made, such as in car wrecks. Sometimes our illnesses or confinements may be similar to the lamb's broken leg. They can become times of closeness with God where we find God sustaining or carrying us. In such times we learn a great deal about ourselves as individuals and as human beings. We also learn more about God and the Giving One's faithful love toward us. Then, even in our circumstances, we can praise God for God's uplifting presence.

While God allows adversities, the Ever-loving One also promises to be with us; we are not alone. There will be gifts in the midst of our difficult times. We can be well acquainted with grief and sadness and still have joy. We can have loss and still be thankful for what we have. Illness can be an opportunity to redefine our living and bring fuller life into our midst. It is wise for us to slow down and rest against a tree, to take the time to look around for God's presence and provision in our windows of opportunity.

I'm writing this at the end of a whirlwind trip. Though I had just visited my dad a week earlier, he had suffered a marked decline; and I wanted to go see him. Whether I fly or drive, traveling the 400 miles that separate us is expensive. Since this was not an emergency, flying was out of the question. As it turned out, my best friend Janet also needed to go to Oklahoma but to a different area of the state. Prayerfully and thoughtfully we came up with a workable plan. We traveled 991 miles in 51 hours. We saw her dad and played nine holes of golf with him. We visited a dear friend and her husband, who was hospitalized, and took her to lunch afterward. Janet took care of her photography business, and I visited with some old friends. We spent time with my dad, celebrated Janet's son's twenty-second birthday, and inhaled the beauty of early October all in one trip!

In a way it was extravagant—991 miles in 51 hours. But the trip was therapeutic. I was able to laugh and to visit with people, be with my dad, play golf, dine well, and have a good, healing change. The trip, conceived in grief by the catalyst of my dad's declining condition, became a vehicle for joy. We were able to take advantage of the opportunities and make the best of each situation.

God is with us in all times, a very present help for us in times of trouble. Our Sustainer is worthy of our worship and praise. Let us enter God's gates with thanksgiving and God's courts with praise, for our Maker's steadfast love endures forever and calls forth in us gladness and thanksgiving.

PRAYER SUGGESTION

Be alert for signs of God's presence in your circumstances. Which people in your life are blessings? What surprises have you experienced, such as unexpected money or insurance coming through just at the right time? What books have you read that lifted your spirit? Perhaps God is upholding you, bracing you from the full reality of your situation. Look where God is reaching out to you, and then offer back to God a gift of thanksgiving. This can be in the form of a prayer, a special act of kindness for someone, or a thank-you note. Express thanksgiving in whatever way seems most natural.

PRAYER

God of dance and laughter,
*   guide our hearts in thanksgiving and praise.*
We give thanks to you and bless your holy name,
*   for your love and faithfulness endure forever.*
You lift us up from our dejection.
You move us through our sadness.
You touch our lives with beauty and joy.
You open windows to bring us life.
We praise you, now and always. May everyone give you
*   praise! Amen.*

THE LAW OF
SOWING AND REAPING

Those who go out weeping, bearing the seed for sowing,
shall come home with shouts of joy, carrying their sheaves.
Psalm 126:7

I remember the day a friend of mine first referred to God as the great Gardener. I thought, *What a wonderful image, God helping to cultivate our lives as a gardener tends plants.* Certainly the parables of Jesus are rich with farming images. One is the parable of the sower, found in the Gospels of Matthew, Mark, and Luke. In this story a farmer goes out to sow seeds; he throws them on the path, in the rocks, among the thorns, and on good soil.

The seeds that hit the path get trampled underfoot and eaten by the birds of the air. Those that fall in the rocks grow up but quickly wither because of a lack of moisture. The seeds that fall among the thorns grow up but are choked out by the thorns. The lucky seeds that fall into the good soil yield a hundredfold.[1] Jesus says that for us to be like the seeds that fall on good soil, we must hold fast with an honest and good heart, bearing fruit with patient endurance (Luke 8:15).

We can respond to illness or caregiving demands in four similar ways. First, we can respond by being asleep to our demands. We stay in denial and oblivion and miss death because we look away. Second, we can put up a valiant but short-lived effort to encounter life head-on. The effort falls short because we do not nurture ourselves. We do not engage in activities that strengthen us and help us stay centered.

Third, we sometimes find ourselves responding pretty well, then suddenly something goes wrong, and we cannot or do not process it. As a result, much of the healthy living that we were able to do gets choked out. And finally, we can find ourselves in circumstances where we have everything we need and are able to have a good death or survive an important death.

Sowing and reaping is a spiritual principle. Knowing this principle can give us hope in the midst of tears.

PSALM 126

When the LORD restored the fortunes of Zion,
 we were like those who dream.
Then our mouth was filled with laughter,
 and our tongue with shouts of joy;
  then it was said among the nations,
  "The LORD has done great things for them."
The LORD has done great things for us, and we rejoiced.

Restore our fortunes, O LORD,
 like the watercourses in the Negeb.
May those who sow in tears reap with shouts of joy.
Those who go out weeping, bearing the seed for sowing,
 shall come home with shouts of joy, carrying their
 sheaves.

May had a good year in 1998: Her breast cancer went into remission. All the worry and work in healing, all the spent emotions and stacked bills, faded into the background as she and her family celebrated life anew each day. It is wonderful when we are able to overcome a devastating disease. All the hard living in the midst of weeping is over; now come the shouts of joy!

May's family members resembled people waking from a dream—they seemed confused and overcome as they journeyed out of their collective nightmare into the light of health. Finally all their prayers had been answered! They were exhausted and overjoyed.

It would be nice to end my illustration here with physical life the winner, but that would not be reality. Like all humans, who die, May's day came three years later. She would be the first to tell you that she richly enjoyed and fully lived the intervening years before her second bout with cancer. But during her last months, many tears were sown. When you love someone, you hate to give up that person. Life is a gift, and letting go of our families, friends, pets, accomplishments, interests, and possessions is hard.

Though May knew the day would come when she would have to face death, she wished it could be years off so she could see her grandchildren graduate from college and marry. Her family and friends wanted to enjoy many more years of her presence and memories. The tears they shed reflected their grief and loss. But again there came a day of rejoicing. When May finally died, there was relief and rejoicing that she was freed from the pain and the brokenness of her body.

May's family and friends did not shout for joy as they did at her remission. Yet they shared a silent joy because May was united with her Lord and the loved ones who had gone before her, and also because they had completed a difficult job well. They had given May wonderful care and attention, and they could be proud of their caregiving. The dying process, with all of the family gathered, had yielded more than a few memorable moments, which brought healing laughter to the family.

Caregiving and surrendering life are not the kinds of seeds we want to sow. Fortunately, the law of sowing and reaping applies anyway, and good can be brought from every loss, even the loss of life. One of the greatest blessings that May's family reaped—and this is true of my family as well—is the wonderful quality time shared with siblings, cousins, and other family and friends during the loved one's illness.

During the time my mother was dying, my sister and brother and I figured that we spent more time together than we had since my brother had gone off to college! It was a gift of holy time. Though it was a time of weeping and sowing seeds with tears, there was also an element of joy in the marvelous sheaves we reaped. May you be blessed a hundredfold in your living and in your dying.

Spend a few minutes quieting yourself. Find a comfortable position and think about your situation. In what areas are you sowing tears? Spend a few minutes on this question. Sometimes we have grief and sadness about losses that we don't consciously acknowledge. We must reflect on such a question in the space of silence to hear a deeper voice within us.

Once you identify seeds of weeping, reflect on this question: What possible sheaves of joy might result? Do what you can to make these things happen.

PRAYER

O God of power and might,
Giver of life and Conqueror of death,
Hear our prayers.
Do not let our tears fall empty to the ground.
Do not let them be in vain,
But bring forth from the tear-soaked land a harvest of
*   hundredfold.*
Fill our hearts with hopeful joy. Amen.

Even though I walk through the
valley of the shadow of death,
I fear no evil; . . .
you anoint my head with oil;
my cup overflows.

Psalm 23:4-5

PART FOUR

The Shepherd's Anointing Sustains Us

GOD'S LOVE ENDURES FOREVER

─────────

O give thanks to the LORD, for he is good,
for his steadfast love endures forever.
Psalm 136:1

For probably a year I passed Ron in the halls and occasionally interacted with him in meetings. Every time we greeted each other and I asked, "How are you?" he gave me the same response: "Fantastic!"

Finally my curiosity got the best of me. Sitting in his office, I asked him how he could always say so enthusiastically that he was fantastic. Ron told me that six years before, a tumor had been removed from his brain. Since he awoke from that surgery, he feels fantastic simply because he is alive.

Listening to Ron talk, I realized that he knew God loved and treasured him. Ron felt he had been given another opportunity to fully live his life, so no matter what the day brought, life was a gift and he was fantastic.

PSALM 136:1-9, 23-26

O give thanks to the LORD, for he is good,
    for his steadfast love endures forever.
O give thanks to the God of gods,
    for his steadfast love endures forever.
O give thanks to the Lord of lords,
    for his steadfast love endures forever;
who alone does great wonders,
    for his steadfast love endures forever;

who by understanding made the heavens,
    for his steadfast love endures forever;
who spread out the earth on the waters,
    for his steadfast love endures forever;
who made the great lights,
    for his steadfast love endures forever;
the sun to rule over the day,
    for his steadfast love endures forever;
the moon and stars to rule over the night,
    for his steadfast love endures forever;

. . . .

It is he who remembered us in our low estate,
    for his steadfast love endures forever;
and rescued us from our foes,
    for his steadfast love endures forever;
who gives food to all flesh,
    for his steadfast love endures forever.

O give thanks to the God of heaven,
    for his steadfast love endures forever.

The psalmist recognizes the source of all the good that surrounds us: God's steadfast love. It is this enduring love that makes the sun and moon to rule the day and night. This love also gives food to all flesh and rescues us regardless of our low estate. God's steadfast love endures forever, and we are the recipients of this everlasting love.

Where can we go in our own lives to look for this steadfast love of the Lord that endures forever? Here are three clues for searching: knowing God's disposition, looking for God's fingerprints, and nurturing a grateful attitude.

Probably the most popular Christian song is "Amazing Grace." John Newton, a slave trader turned evangelical minister, wrote it. His life bore the unmistakable print of divine transformation.

Grace first and foremost expresses God's disposition of love toward us. We can also understand grace as God's power in us to do what we cannot do for ourselves. God's grace is amazing because it is based on God's steadfast love, not on what we do. We cannot earn it or merit it; God's love is a free gift. If we are going to find God's steadfast love in our lives, our search begins with the willingness to believe that God loves us with an everlasting, steadfast love.

Armed with the knowledge of God's amazing grace for us, we look for situations where the Lord has extended grace to us. We look for God's fingerprints. As I shared in the meditation on Psalm 121, when I received the call from my sister about our father's second stroke, I was at the airport holding an airline voucher for twenty-five dollars over the amount of the round-trip ticket to Oklahoma City. Those two realities convinced me of God's presence in the midst of my situation. The ticket and the timing showed God's fingerprints to me.

The third thing we can do is to nurture an attitude of gratefulness for God's grace in our lives. In seminary a few of my international friends from Africa told me that on the first day of each month, the people give thanks to God for all of their gifts, but they do not ask God for anything. For instance, they thank God for providing food, but they do not ask God to bless it. I have celebrated the first of the month this way. It sounds easy, but if you try all day to be thankful as you talk to God, you will catch yourself asking for things. Asking seems to be automatic for us. On the other hand, when we practice being grateful, we tend to see more and more things for which to be grateful. In our gratitude, we know the steadfast, enduring love of the Lord.

Some of us may feel that God loves other people but not us. The truth is, God loves everyone equally. Only God is fully impartial in loving. Frequently we do not accept God's love because we will not accept God's forgiveness of our mistakes and sins. Accepting God's forgiveness means that we must forgive ourselves.

Others of us may look at our life's circumstances and know that we have come out on the short end of the stick. Some of us were born into economically deprived situations. Some of us were born to abusive parents. Life isn't fair; God never said it was. The gift that nurtures our life is God's grace, God's love that seeks us and meets us where we are and strives to bring healing and wholeness into our lives.

Unquestionably Ron knew the Lord's steadfast love. A devout believer, he knew that when he died he would go to heaven. Like many of us who are confident in God's plans for us, Ron, however, was not anxious to get to the next life. He had a wife, children, family, and friends. He wanted to continue to savor this marvelous gift of life. He wanted to live to the nice ripe age of eighty.

Sometimes Christians feel it is wrong to say we believe in heaven and God's love for us and yet hold to life here and now. There is nothing wrong with this. This life is a gift, not just a path to the next life. We do best when we live as those prepared to die and die as those prepared to live, so that living or dying, we are actively present in the moment. We can be ready to die and still be living life here. At some point we all have to surrender our lives to death, for death represents our final surrender of ourselves to God's steadfast, enduring love.

I had a beautiful experience yesterday. I visited a new patient, a lovely woman of eighty-nine years. While recovering from a heart attack, she had a massive stroke. She could not open her eyes, but she could speak clearly and hear. Her sudden blindness required an enormous adjustment to overcome her fear and begin to cope with her new reality. We connected immediately. She grasped my hand tightly. I asked her if she would like prayer, and she responded, "Oh yes," and pulled my hand to her heart. I shared Psalms 121 and 23, as well as part of Psalm 139, in prayer. A holiness surrounded us. She whispered, "It is good to remember that we are in God's love." "You are so right," I replied and smiled as I watched the transformation in her countenance.

It is marvelous how statements of faith can reassure another. If this brave soul was able to find comfort in the declaration of God's steadfast and enduring love for us, I pray that you too will hear the cry of the psalmist, "O give thanks to the LORD, for he is good, / for his steadfast love endures forever."

PRAYER SUGGESTION

Think of a time when you have known the steadfast love of the Lord. Savor the fullness of that memory.

Prayer

O give thanks to the Lord, for he is good and his steadfast love endures forever.

O give thanks to our God, who makes the sun rule the day and the moon guide the night.

O give thanks to our creative God, who splashes the skies with brilliant colors to announce the beginning and ending of day and night.

Come to us, God of enduring love; come to us in our misery and in our joy.

Splash our lives with your grace—your amazing grace that enlivens our lives.

O God, we give you thanks for all of our blessings.

We give thanks to you for grace.

We give thanks to you for you.

We give thanks to you that we have the wisdom to know to give thanks.

Thanks! Amen.

FINDING JOY
IN A FOREIGN LAND

How could we sing the LORD's song in a foreign land?
Psalm 137:4

My visits with Vickie made me feel helpless. The first time I walked away from her house, I cried. The mother of five children, Vickie was forty-one and suffered from brain cancer. She had two children, ages eleven and fourteen, who were still at home. You could tell Vickie had once been beautiful, but now cancer had partially shrunk one side of her face and closed one eye. The big difficulty I had in visiting Vickie was her lack of outward emotional reaction. She usually answered questions with one or two words, and she rarely asked questions or commented on anything. Her situation and my sense of inadequacy in helping her grieved me deeply.

Whenever I called Vickie to ask if she would like a visit, she always said yes. Communicating with her was challenging because her speech was hard to understand, though she could hear herself clearly (an added frustration for her). I felt our visits were awkward and that I offered her little. I spoke with other members of Vickie's team, and they had the same experience. I prayed fervently for a way to help Vickie and her family.

When we are with seriously ill people, it's easy to feel useless or as though we have two left feet. The awkwardness happens in part when we can't make conversation with the person. In these cases we want a defined task to do, but we may or may not get one. Sitting in silence can be awkward. But as caregivers we need to hang on until an opportunity comes to be of service.

The ill person also feels awkward. No one is in more foreign territory than seriously ill persons. Their dreams are crashing all around them, and they know they are in a process; they just don't know how it will turn out. It is a painful and uprooting experience, but by faith they can be rooted in the strength of God and endure the radical change of illness.

PSALM 137:1-4

By the rivers of Babylon—
>   there we sat down and there we wept when we
>   remembered Zion.
On the willows there we hung up our harps.
For there our captors asked us for songs,
>   and our tormentors asked for mirth, saying,
"Sing us one of the songs of Zion!"

How could we sing the LORD's song in a foreign land?

Psalm 137 is a psalm of intense lament. In the sixth century before Christ, Babylonian armies destroyed Israel. In 586 B.C.E. Jerusalem was sacked and her leaders taken away into captivity in Babylon. The people of Jerusalem mourned the loss of their homeland, especially their Temple, the dwelling place of God. They had praised and worshiped God at Zion. When this psalm was written, not only had the Temple been destroyed and the leaders of Jerusalem taken captive to another country, but their captors also tormented them about their loss and grief.

The songs of Zion mentioned in verse 3 are songs about the glory and majesty of God. Israel's captors take pleasure in tormenting them. I can imagine them taunting: "Sing to us one of the songs of Zion; sing to us about your mighty God who delivered you into our hands. Ha! Your God is not so mighty! Where are your songs now? Where is this awesome God? You pathetic people." What great sorrow must have filled the Israelites' hearts as they sat downcast and dejected by the rivers of Babylon, longing for their home. They even hung their harps in the willow trees, for they did not have songs of might and glory to sing to their God. Their home was destroyed.

How could they sing the Lord's songs in a foreign land? How could they sing of God's awesomeness?

How much like Israel we can feel when illness and caregiving destroy our lives and enchain us with restrictions. How can we sing songs of joy when we are suffering so? Our harps may be the cars we can no longer drive, the places where we can no longer travel. Our harps may be our kitchens that stare us in the face though we cannot enter them to cook, or our yards that beckon though we can no longer tend them. A great deal of sorrow accompanies illness. Some days I just weep while traveling home from work.

I am blessed to be able to sing the Lord's song most of the time. The roots of my faith go deep enough to sustain me during the overwhelming sorrowful and frightening times of my life. My faith is fed and stirred by remembering. First, I remember that all of the land is the Lord's. There is nowhere we can go to escape God's grace and love—nowhere. So even if the land is foreign to me, it is not to God, and remembering that gives me hope.

Second, I stir up good memories by thinking of times when I felt God's presence or the healing love of another person. There is a sense in which memories can counter other experiences by bringing warmth to our hearts and souls. Sometimes I intentionally recall childhood memories of freedom. They bring a smile to my heart when I am working. Our experiences in life tend to balance each other, with the good times making the bad bearable.

The Lord answered my prayer about Vickie and gave me opportunities to help her. One opportunity came during her stay at Christopher House. She went in on a Friday afternoon. Her field nurse called and left me a message saying that Vickie felt depressed about having to go to Christopher House. The nurse said she would appreciate my going to see Vickie, since Vickie liked me. I was amazed to hear that Vickie liked me, since I felt I had done so little for her.

I arrived shortly after 8 P.M. Vickie felt miserable, but she had just started watching a movie on TV and obviously she was going to be awake for a while. I decided to settle in and watch the movie with her. Acting intuitively, I took her hand and held it—she had long slender fingers on a beautiful hand. At one point in the movie she turned to me and simply said, "Thank you for being with me." That made my night. I was thrilled to have been helpful to her. Together that night we found the Lord's song in a foreign land. I kissed her good-bye when I left. From that time on, she always made a subtle gesture when I was leaving to let me know she wanted her kiss.

Some of us will be able by faith to sing the Lord's song in the land of the shadow of death. Others of us will not be able to overcome our sorrow and grief. In both cases, God will love us equally. God will not give up on us, especially when we are in a foreign land.

Prayer Suggestion

What is your favorite hymn or other song of faith? Sing or play the song, and enjoy the encouragement that comes from singing songs of faith.

Prayer

O God, help us. It is frightening to find ourselves in a
*   foreign land—bereft, alone.*
O God, be near us; your home seems so far away.
Help us, Lord, help us.
Bring back the memory of your songs in our heart.
Warm us and bring music back into our lives.
May the songs break the bonds of the suffering that we
*   bear. Amen.*

WHAT BEST
NOURISHES YOU?

They are like trees planted by streams of water,
which yield their fruit in its season,
and their leaves do not wither.
In all that they do, they prosper.

Psalm 1:3

There is a world of difference between the statements *I have to* and *I get to.*
The first statement implies that since I have to do it, I just may not enjoy
it. From the start I have a negative, or at least jaundiced, attitude. On the other
hand, saying "I get to" implies an opportunity. If something is a blessing, we
approach it with a positive attitude; we usually don't mind doing it.

Sometimes we get confused between our "have tos" and our "get tos." For
instance, going to the grocery story or the pharmacy becomes a "have to,"
when in reality the idea that we can go and easily get what we need is a great
blessing. That reality can brighten our going so we can see it as a "get to"
rather than as a "have to."

One of the most wonderful parts of life is that we get to grow spiritually
and emotionally. We can undertake activities that will definitely make a difference in our lives. The odd thing is that we frequently view these opportunities for growth as "have tos"; what could be a pleasure becomes a chore
simply because of our attitude toward it. Or worse yet, our attitude prevents
us from even undertaking the activity. Our perspective can make all the difference in the world.

PSALM 1:1-3

Happy are those
    who do not follow the advice of the wicked,
    or take the path that sinners tread,
    or sit in the seat of scoffers;
but their delight is in the law of the LORD,
    and on his law they meditate day and night.

They are like trees planted by streams of water,
    which yield their fruit in its season,
    and their leaves do not wither.
In all that they do, they prosper.

The very first psalm contrasts two groups of people. One group is the scoffers, the wicked, and the sinners. These people depart from God's ways. The other group is God's righteous, the ones who please God by how they respond. The second group's attitude is that they are "happy." These people follow God's law, not because they have to, but because doing so is a delight to them. On God's law they mediate day and night. The law here is not the observance of rules and regulations but the guidance and direction of God in their lives.

The psalmist uses a metaphor of a tree to bring home his point. Those who seek and follow God are like trees planted by streams of water. They get all the water they need, and they bear good fruit and prosper. This metaphor is used elsewhere in scripture too. My favorite passage is from Jeremiah:

Blessed are those who trust in the LORD,
    whose trust is the LORD.
They shall be like a tree planted by water,
    sending out its roots by the stream.
It shall not fear when heat comes,
    and its leaves shall stay green;
    in the year of drought it is not anxious,
and it does not cease to bear fruit. (Jer. 17:7-8)

Jeremiah clarifies that the fundamental relationship between God and people who are like healthy trees is that they trust God even when the heat and the drought come.

For those of us faced with illness, now is when we need our faith. It is now that we need a trust in God that will carry us through our illness. For those of us faced with a loved one who is ill, now is when we need our faith. It is now that we need to seek God and trust that God's guidance will carry us all through the experience. If our roots are not down by living waters, they need to be.

Meeting Dorothy was a gift. Her father was dying of cancer. He had been misdiagnosed and had gone untreated for several years. By the time Dorothy moved back home and took him to another facility that properly diagnosed his cancer, it was too late to cure him. Dorothy, like all of her family, was angry and upset. But unlike her family, Dorothy had significantly more reason for her emotions. Though only in her mid-forties, she too had been misdiagnosed with cancer five years before by the clinic she attended. She too had finally gone to another hospital facility in another town and discovered her disease. Fortunately, she found her cancer early enough that it was treatable and is now in remission.

When I first met Dorothy and her family, she did not tell me the story of their misdiagnoses and their bouts with cancer. No, when I first met Dorothy she talked with me about her faith. Her dad was a Baptist, and her mother a Methodist. She told me right off that she could not settle for her mother's or her father's religion. Their faith would not help her or get her into heaven. She had to find her own faith, her own walk with God. She had tried all sorts of churches from Catholic to Full Gospel Fellowship. She had even studied other religions before she found God, before she found her streams of living water where she could set down her roots. Now her faith was like a full-grown tree; her leaves did not wither from fear or cancer. She had survived her own bout with death; she would survive her father's. And the branches of her tree would give some solace and protection to her family.

Whenever I visited Dorothy, the power of faith always came up in the conversation. She knew that to thrive in her faith she had to be "prayed up." In other words, she had to have a strong, active relationship with God so that when the storms or drought came, she could stand firm in her trust in the Lord. She was the first one to share with you her faith and her journey. By remembering, she recalled the power of grace that had sustained her.

I was deeply touched some years ago by the story of a man whose wife was seriously ill. For several evenings a convenience store owner had noticed a car sitting out front. This information became important later when the store was robbed. On the day of the robbery, the same car had appeared in front of the store. As the police investigated the crime, they approached the car and asked the man why he parked in that spot every afternoon.

The man explained that his wife was seriously ill in the hospital. Their farm was some 150 miles away, and the man was beset with grief and worry. He went on to tell the policeman that he did not spend much time in church buildings, but the reason he came here each evening was because of the church across the street. His hotel was just a few blocks away, and he had discovered that late in the afternoon sunlight hit the church's stained glass windows. For some reason their beauty filled him with peace. So each day at this time he left the hospital and came to sit here in his car for as long as the light lasted. Those minutes were the only peaceful time he had each day, for the rest of his time was crowded with worry and concern.

This man had found a stream of living water to nurture his soul and his spirit. The streams are out there for all of us. It is our work to discover them and to drink from their nurturing waters. This is a blessing that we get to do.

PRAYER SUGGESTION

What best nourishes you? What do you enjoy most? Write or journal, play or sing music, do art of any kind or look at art, go for a long meditative walk or just out into nature, sit in your yard and reflect or weed a garden, read scripture or a good book, offer your services to others, or do whatever works for you to make you aware of God's presence. The idea is to find ways to spend time with God that are a delight for you—a "get to" experience rather than a "have to." Let these activities nurture your faith.

PRAYER

*O God, we are all sinners. We all fall short of your desires
for us. Yet you meet each of us with love, forgiveness,
and acceptance.*

Help us to delight in you and in our faith.

*Help us to develop the type of faith that will give us deep
roots.*

*Help us to be planted by streams of living waters, nurturing
our relationship with you so that when the heat and
droughts of our lives come, our trust in you will carry
us through.*

In your holy name we pray. Amen.

KEEP THE FAITH

I kept my faith, even when I said,
"I am greatly afflicted."
Psalm 116:10

As a hospice worker I deal with end-of-life care for a number of different people at the same time. Like all workers in this field, I have regular grief that I must deal with. Recently I returned home from visiting my dad. I was dealing with his grief and mine, as well as undergoing significant changes in other areas of my life. It was a time of daily walking in trust and faith. It was also a time of uncertainty and fear.

Within less than twenty-four hours after arriving home from visiting my dad, I lost three patients to death. Two deaths jolted me because they were untimely and in that sense unexpected. One of the patients I had been with for eight months. I arrived a few minutes after he died, following an unbearably frustrating trip trying to get to our inpatient unit before his death. When I walked into the room, his grieving wife and I just held each other and cried. My grief buckets were full, and for my own well-being they had to be emptied.

From time to time we all experience emotional buildup like water behind a dam. Since all losses create grief, a new grief can tap into our existing sources of unprocessed or unhealed grief. Experiencing several setbacks or sources of grief in a short time frame can challenge the strength of our faith. The writer of Psalm 116 had apparently just gone through a time of illness in the shadow of death.

I love the LORD, because he has heard
    my voice and my supplications.
Because he inclined his ear to me,
    therefore I will call on him as long as I live.

The snares of death encompassed me;
    the pangs of Sheol laid hold on me;
    I suffered distress and anguish.
Then I called on the name of the LORD:
    "O LORD, I pray, save my life!"

Gracious is the LORD, and righteous;
    our God is merciful.
The LORD protects the simple;
    when I was brought low, he saved me.
Return, O my soul, to your rest,
    for the LORD has dealt bountifully with you.

For you have delivered my soul from death,
    my eyes from tears,
    my feet from stumbling.
I walk before the LORD in the land of the living.
I kept my faith, even when I said,
    "I am greatly afflicted";
I said in my consternation,
    "Everyone is a liar."

What shall I return to the LORD for all his bounty to me?
I will lift up the cup of salvation
    and call on the name of the LORD,
I will pay my vows to the LORD

in the presence of all his people.
Precious in the sight of the LORD
   is the death of his faithful ones.
O LORD, I am your servant;
   I am your servant, the child of your serving girl.
   You have loosed my bonds.
I will offer to you a thanksgiving sacrifice
   and call on the name of the LORD.
I will pay my vows to the LORD
   in the presence of all his people,
   in the courts of the house of the LORD,
   in your midst, O Jerusalem.
Praise the LORD!

Shortly before I began seminary, my mother and I had a conversation about faith. She asked me if faith was a gift. Yes, I replied. Then she asked me, "How can a person be faulted if he or she does not have enough faith?"

My mother taught me that the issue of faith was much more complicated than I had thought. Faith is a gift in that we respond to God's unmerited love. The fact that we can believe and trust is a gift. But faith is also our response. It involves active belief and confident trust of those we love, as well as ourselves, into God's care. Maintaining our faith in times of great trials can be hard work.

The psalmist loves God because he has been rescued from the snares of death. He tells his soul to rest easy because God has dealt bountifully with him. God has delivered his soul from death, his eyes from tears, and his feet from stumbling. The image he creates is a beautiful one: "I walk before the LORD in the land of the living." The psalmist's saving experience has fueled his faith anew, and he is ready to lift up the cup of salvation and pay his vows to the Lord.

According to the psalmist, his faith was active in the midst of his turmoil, for he states, "I kept my faith, even when I said, / 'I am greatly afflicted.'" Illness and its complications can challenge our faith. We are more complex and more frail than we imagine. We can feel confident, go to sleep, and wake up in an entirely different situation. It is not surprising that our faith gets challenged.

One of the horrors I witness in my hospice work is how often people experience numerous traumas and sources of deep grief. Such was the case with Toni. Her father died in December. In February she was diagnosed with cancer. Soon after that, three close relatives were also diagnosed with cancer. By January of the next year all three had died. She could not believe they were diagnosed after she was and yet died before her. In a thirteen-month period, she suffered four significant losses, as well as the erosion of her own health.

The deaths were a devastating blow to Toni. The grief of the last death seemed to break her spirit, and she became deeply depressed. The worst part for Toni was having "survivor guilt" in the midst of living daily with her own terminal cancer. To some extent the deaths undercut the confidence of her faith because their grief crushed her hope for a time.

Nevertheless, Toni was able to rally her faith in God's love and ultimate plans for her. For a brief period her love for her family allowed her to rebound, but the multiple losses took a harsh toll on her joy; she died within a month. She left three children with families who now must lean on their own beliefs and hopes to keep their faith going. Fortunately they have several resources that encourage their faith and healing.

At some time we all must "keep the faith" when it looks like we are losing the war. I hope we will all be able to declare with the psalmist, "I kept my faith, even when I said, / 'I am greatly afflicted.'"

PRAYER SUGGESTION

One of my regular practices to help wash away my grief is to experience my showers not just physically but also spiritually and emotionally. As the water rinses over me, I allow my frustrations, fears, and grief to wash right off me too. I trust that the One who made the water is on my side and is cleansing me. When my heart is lightened, I give thanks for the cleansing. Try it and see if it helps lighten your load a little . If you don't have a shower, use a container to pour bath water over your head for the same cleansing effect.

PRAYER

God of us all, your love never ends, and because of this we are greatly blessed. But the natural world you created has beginnings and endings. And at times it is hard for us to have strong faith when those around us are being stricken.

Strengthen our faith, O Lord. Give us such faith that by day and by night we can without question entrust all those we love into your steadfast caring.

Thank you for the gift of faith that you have given us. Put people in our lives to encourage our faith and keep us on your path. Amen.

HEALING DESPITE DISEASE

Those who have clean hands and pure hearts. . . .
They will receive blessing from the LORD,
and vindication from the God of their salvation.
Psalm 24:4-5

It is ironic that some experiences that we consider most unique are often the very experiences we share with others. For instance, someone may think that he or she is the only person at a gathering who is self-conscious, yet others feel the same way. Or we may think that we are the only ones in the family who wish Uncle Mike would just go ahead and die. But we probably are not. We tend to be aware of our feelings and less attuned to others' feelings.

Death is an equalizer—it comes to all people. While there are many commonalities in the experience of death, each person's death is as unique as his or her birth. It is a solo experience.

Dying, on the other hand, is a process that can involve many people and may take place over a considerable period of time. During the dying process we revisit areas of our life that have a lot of energy connected with them. These can be safe, pleasant memories such as a period in childhood, or they can be problematic times we did not resolve. In the dying process we let go of the material world and prepare to enter an entirely new existence. While disease may be the path to our bodily destruction, it can also be a path of healing for ourselves and for others around us.

PSALM 24:1-6

The earth is the LORD's and all that is in it,
    the world, and those who live in it;

for he has founded it on the seas,
and established it on the rivers.

Who shall ascend the hill of the LORD?
And who shall stand in his holy place?
Those who have clean hands and pure hearts,
who do not lift up their souls to what is false,
and do not swear deceitfully.
They will receive blessing from the LORD,
and vindication from the God of their salvation.
Such is the company of those who seek him,
who seek the face of the God of Jacob.

The psalmist begins with a declaration that the earth is the Lord's, and so is everything that is in it. He then immediately raises the questions: Who can be in God's presence? Who can stand in God's holy place? The psalmist replies that it is those who have clean hands and pure hearts and are not deceitful or false. I daresay that many of us might discard ourselves from God's presence because of the intimate knowledge we have of ourselves! We know that our hearts are not pure. We know that we have been deceitful to ourselves, as well as to others. How then can we stand in God's holy place?

All of us have inclinations to think or do things that are unhelpful or detrimental to others and ourselves. In evaluating ourselves, we need to be mindful that God knows how we are made. After the flood, when God made a covenant to never again destroy the earth by water, he did so because, "The inclination of the human heart is evil from youth" (Gen. 8:21). This inclination is a part of being human; all people's hearts are a bit devious. However, during the course of life we are given many opportunities to respond in love or out of lesser motives. These are the ways, the paths we choose to walk, for which we are accountable. How we give of ourselves and use our resources will determine the blessings or the vindications that we will receive.

At times God seems to allow people to have some say-so about when they will die. For instance, people will hang on to life by a thread until a certain person arrives or some task is completed. I know of at least a dozen cases where hospice patients clung to life just long enough to receive words of forgiveness and love. One such instance happened on a Saturday. Dolly's mother, who lived with her, was actively dying. I gathered with the family around the kitchen table while the patient was some twelve feet away in an adjoining living room. The patient had been in a coma for over a week, and her nurses could not comprehend how she was still alive.

After about two and a half hours of talking, we uncovered some serious problems in the family. The heart of the matter was that Dolly's mother was pregnant with her before she got married. On some level her mother had held this against her only child, and Dolly never received the nurture or love that she should have. Years later this same mother helped raise one of Dolly's daughters. Dolly's mother loved and cuddled her grandchild and gave her everything she had denied Dolly. Understandably, this caused problems with all the people involved. The question now was, how did the family want to proceed? Did they love one other? Did they want to do the work, the therapy or counseling, necessary to work through their problems and liberate this love? The answer to both questions was yes.

After a plan was worked out, we gathered around Dolly's mother's hospital bed for prayer. Each person present said her peace with the dying woman and lifted up what she was most thankful for about her. When this was over, Dolly and her daughter tearfully explained to the dying woman that they loved each other and they were going to take concrete steps to resolve their problems. It was a powerful and emotional time.

When the prayer was over, I noticed that the patient began breathing differently. Her children went to get some medicines, and I went home. About fifteen minutes after I left the house, the patient died. Following the pronouncement of death by our nurse, the family requested that I come back. When I got there, I found tears of relief, sadness, and joy. Without a doubt, the family felt that the patient had been lingering for a resolution of the huge problem she had helped to create. The family had sought my presence in an attempt to uncover what was still keeping her alive. It seems that once the conflict was uncovered and the honest resolution told to the patient, she was released from her broken body.

In her dying the patient's family had found a path for healing and life. To never have addressed the hurt Dolly felt would have been deceitful to herself and false to her family. Trying to resolve the problems and opening the door for love was a responsible action God honored by blessing the family.

The promise of the psalmist is that God will bless those with clean hands and a pure heart. Opening our hearts and looking at their contents in the light of God begins the process. Asking and giving forgiveness cleans and purifies our hearts.

Whether you are an ill person or helping to care for someone who is, now is an excellent time to examine your heart and your life. Then take what action you can to bring love and healing to the situation. Do not beat up on yourself for the characteristics you cannot change, but do take the actions you can to clean your hands and purify your heart.

PRAYER SUGGESTION

Where can you use God's healing—in something you experienced during your childhood? in your marriage? in accepting yourself? Spend some time examining your heart; then take the appropriate actions to seek forgiveness and healing for yourself and for others involved.

PRAYER

O God, it gets so confusing at times.
We want to be perfect, but we can't be. We want to always
do what is right, but we can't. Sometimes we hide
things for fear others will know and think we are
terrible people.
Help us to see into our devious hearts.
Give us the faith and courage to change what we can, to
seek clean hands and a pure heart.
Enfold us in your healing love, and help us to better love
others. Amen.

REJOICE IN YOUR FAITH

Happy are those whose strength is in you,
in whose heart are the highways to Zion.
Psalm 84:5

Fifty-five-year-old Maggie had lived two years longer than her doctors had thought she would. One reason her doctors think she did so well was because Maggie continued to embrace life as fully as she could despite her cancer. An avid scuba diver, she did not her battle with cancer end her regular trips. Twice a year she and her husband continued going to their favorite place in Mexico to dive. Sometimes Maggie was too ill to dive, but she spent healing time reading, reflecting, and just enjoying the beach.

A well-adjusted woman, she and her husband of thirty-five years shared a deep relationship as lovers, friends, and coworkers. During her fifty-five years, Maggie's wholeness and spirituality touched hundreds of people. She was famous for her indomitable strength and kindness. Though she died young, she lived a full life. Neither she nor her husband had any regrets.

PSALM 84

How lovely is your dwelling place,
    O LORD of hosts!
My soul longs, indeed it faints
    for the courts of the LORD;
my heart and my flesh sing for joy to the living God.

Even the sparrow finds a home, and the swallow a nest for
    herself,

where she may lay her young,
at your altars, O LORD of hosts,
    my King and my God.
Happy are those who live in your house, ever singing your
    praise.

Happy are those whose strength is in you,
    in whose heart are the highways to Zion.
As they go through the valley of Baca
    they make it a place of springs;
    the early rain also covers it with pools.
They go from strength to strength;
    the God of gods will be seen in Zion.

O LORD God of hosts, hear my prayer;
    give ear, O God of Jacob!

Behold our shield, O God;
    look on the face of your anointed.

For a day in your courts is better
    than a thousand elsewhere.
I would rather be a doorkeeper in the house of my God
    than live in the tents of wickedness.
For the LORD God is a sun and shield;
    he bestows favor and honor.
No good thing does the LORD withhold
    from those who walk uprightly.
O LORD of hosts,
    happy is everyone who trusts in you.

This is a psalm about spiritual journey. It has three movements. First, it begins
by speaking about God's dwelling place. It is a lovely place that our souls long

for; indeed our souls faint to be in God's presence. The Creator's home is one in which even the sparrow and the swallow find nests to have their young. It is a safe and nurturing place. No one is unimportant; no one is overlooked. Everyone who lives in God's house is happy!

Second, the traveling section of the psalm begins. Happy are those whose strength is found in God and whose heart becomes a pathway to God. As they travel toward God, they will go through the desert valley of Baca on their way to plush Zion. They will find what they need to continue traveling as they go from strength to strength. God's provision will be sufficient for them and will bring blessing to those around them.

Third, the psalmist asks specifically that God hear his prayer. He confesses that he would rather be a doorkeeper in the house of God than live in the tents of wickedness, for the psalmist knows that a day in God's courts is better than a thousand elsewhere. "No good thing does the LORD withhold / from those who walk uprightly" (that is, with God). He concludes that everyone who trusts in God will be happy. In other words, everyone who hopes in the Lord will find fullness and meaning in life.

Faith carries us through life's difficulties. It is an energizing power that holds us to our Anchor during the storms of life. At the same time, faith holds our heads above the water, even when we cannot feel God's presence. The faith we live encourages those around us. To use another analogy, faith is the power that drives our roots down deeply into the soil. Faith binds us to the earth so that when the winds come and blow (as they do and will), we are sustained and not blown over or away. Faith empowers our souls to be satisfied.

Many people argue about whether quality or quantity of life is more important. In terms of living, quality of life is more important than quantity. As the psalmist concludes, one day in God's courts is better than having a thousand somewhere else. It's better to live a rich, full life and die at fifty-five than to avoid living life and simply exist for eighty years. There are things far worse than death.

Maggie's life was rich and full because of her faith. She held deep beliefs about God and about our purposes here on earth. She knew that relationships mattered the most, and she ordered her priorities. Some 350 to 400 people attended her funeral. Though Maggie's life was short by current standards, it was a powerful and effective life. Those who attended her funeral expressed both great thanksgiving at being touched by her life and great grief at the loss of her physical presence.

For the people of faith, God's home is at the end of this life's journey. In God's courts we will sing praises. So let us embrace this gift of life and live it fully in the knowledge and comfort of God. Let us rejoice in our faith and be content with the number of days we receive.

PRAYER SUGGESTION

In January 1992 I went on a ten-day retreat. At the end of the retreat, I wrote a personal prayer that encapsulated the work I was doing to focus my prayers and express my heart's desires to God. I still say this prayer several times a week. Like the Lord's Prayer, it is a foundational prayer for my spiritual life. I have added other daily prayers, but I have not changed or dropped this one. It is a guiding and directing prayer for me, because each time I pray it I refocus on the most meaningful characteristics of my faith. My prayer goes like this:

> O Lord, my God, you who are the end and the glory of my life,
>   receive my prayer today and bless it. For I will to will
>   your will in every area of my life.

> Strengthen and confirm me, Lord. Make my yes to you a yes
>   and my no to disordered attachments a no.

> Guide me in my journey toward inward and outward simplic-
>   ity, free me from my ego-centeredness; free me from my
>   excesses—especially wasteful spending of money and
>   excessive eating.

> Help me to be a good steward of your mysteries and a faithful
>   minister to you and your flocks.

Above all else, let nothing separate me from your love.

In the words of Saint Francis of Assisi:

> Lord, make me an instrument of your peace.
> Where there is hatred, let me sow love;
> where there is injury, pardon;
> where there is doubt, faith;
> where there is despair, hope;
> where there is darkness, light;
> and where there is sadness, joy.
>
> O Divine Master,
> grant that I may not so much seek
> to be consoled as to console;
> to be understood as to understand,
> to be loved as to love;
> for it is in giving that we receive;
> it is in pardoning that we are pardoned;
> and it is in dying that we are born to eternal life.

I suggest that you take some time to develop your own personal prayer. Make it the prayer of your heart, but also say something about what you believe about God. For instance, when I say, "You are the end and glory of my life," I remind myself that God and God's purposes are more important than me and my purposes. By praying "to will your will," I am asking to embrace what God sends my way; I am also asking that I might be aligned with God's purposes for my life. When I say "let nothing separate me from your love," this is my base prayer. No matter what happens to me in life, the bottom line is that I do not want it to separate me from God's love.

Once you write your prayer, pray it often and memorize it so that whether you are out walking, sitting at a stoplight, standing in a grocery line, or waiting in a doctor's office, you can pray it anywhere at any time. It will turn your heart toward God and reaffirm your deepest beliefs.

PRAYER

Loving One, we long for your presence and for the fullness
of life.
Hear our prayer and strengthen our faith.
Guide us as we journey to our eternal home.
Help us to enjoy the gift of life richly, and allow us to be
blessings to those around us. Amen.

SALVATION FROM OUR TRUE ENEMIES

---

*If it had not been the L*ORD *who was on our side,*
when our enemies attacked us,
then they would have swallowed us up alive,
when their anger was kindled against us;
then the flood would have swept us away,
the torrent would have gone over us;
then over us would have gone the raging waters.
Psalm 124:2-5

While I don't normally think of myself as having enemies, occasionally there are times in my life when enemies exist. Sometimes they are people. But more often than not, my enemies are attitudes, emotions, mind-sets, or institutions. If you had to list your enemies, what would your list look like? Would it include people, emotions, events, or maybe life itself?

To be in touch with our reality is to be a part of the real—to be alive to the life around us. The only way we can live wisely is to know ourselves. Mature living involves knowing oneself—emotions, capabilities, gifts, limitations, and yes, even enemies. Looking inward to our own souls is a part of our life of prayer, with self-examination and reflection at its heart.

There have been many discussions on whether prayer changes God or us. I think it does both. By giving prayer words, we overhear our conversation with God and see both life and ourselves more clearly. I also believe that God ordains prayer with the power to change circumstances. The very fact that we pray confirms our assent to God's activity in our life. Our prayers allow God to respond; they give life to us and welcome God's presence.

In a similar sense, there can be great power in naming our enemies. By doing this, we are able to recognize our true problems and enemies and not let one problem masquerade as another. We can break through our denial and blindness and become better prepared to deal with our real problems. For example, having to live with nagging pain can cause us to see our disease as our sole problem. "Fix the illness, and I'll be fine," we say. In reality, depression and apprehension may be the greater enemies that have driven a wedge between us and our families. With illness, we can easily focus on the physical and dismiss the mental and emotional aspects of life.

In the devotion on Psalm 31, I presented the image of floating on water as a way of surrendering and trusting God's leading in our lives. When I experience enemies, I imagine being out on the sea of life and trying to hold on to an anchor while being swamped by crashing waves. The water breaks over my head, choking me at times. I hang on to my Anchor for dear life, for I have found that where God is, there is help. This is also our psalmist's experience as recorded in Psalm 124.

PSALM 124

If it had not been the LORD who was on our side
    —let Israel now say—
if it had not been the LORD who was on our side,
    when our enemies attacked us,
then they would have swallowed us up alive,
    when their anger was kindled against us;
then the flood would have swept us away,
    the torrent would have gone over us;
then over us would have gone
    the raging waters.

Blessed be the LORD,
    who has not given us as prey to their teeth.
We have escaped like a bird

> from the snare of the fowlers;
>> the snare is broken,
>>> and we have escaped.
>
> Our help is in the name of the LORD,
>> who made heaven and earth.

Without God's presence in our lives, we would perish from despair and death. Most of us have experienced surviving an unbearably difficult time, and then later, in retrospect, wondering how we ever made it. Thank goodness God's grace is with us even when we are not aware of it.

One of the greatest blessings I've had as a chaplain was serving Robert and his family. Our story is truly one of providence. I was on call the weekend after Robert came on service, and his family called for a chaplain. Once there, I discovered that Robert and his wife had recently moved to Austin to be closer to their only child, a daughter. After the move Robert's health had taken a sharp turn for the worse. The couple literally knew no one in Austin except for their daughter's in-laws, who had also recently moved here.

As it turned out, Robert and his wife were lifelong Methodists from Oklahoma City—my hometown and the United Methodist conference in which I am an ordained elder. I knew their home church; I had once preached an Emmaus service in their sanctuary and had served on the team for a Walk to Emmaus held at the church. I even knew their pastor. I was a breath of fresh air to them, a friend and minister from home. Suddenly they no longer felt so alone. The frightening enemy of aloneness came at a vulnerable time in their lives, but it was squelched in part by a new friend from home.

Robert's death was slow and similar to my mother's. It was especially hard because the ending dragged out for so long. I came by almost every day, even on weekends when I was on call and happened to be in their neighborhood. It was a sacred time for all of us, and God clearly orchestrated it for our mutual benefit.

Ephesians is one of my favorite books of the Bible. The prayer in the third chapter is awesome.

I pray that, according to the riches of his glory, he may grant that you may be strengthened in your inner being with power through his Spirit, and that Christ may dwell in your hearts through faith, as you are being rooted and grounded in love. I pray that you may have the power to comprehend, with all the saints, what is the breadth and length and height and depth, and to know the love of Christ that surpasses knowledge, so that you may be filled with all the fullness of God.

Now to him who by the power at work within us is able to accomplish abundantly far more than all we can ask or imagine, to him be glory in the church and in Christ Jesus to all generations, forever and ever. Amen. (Eph. 3:16-21)

God is on our side. Paul's prayer to the Ephesians expresses God's will for us. God desires that we will be strengthened in our inner being by the power of the Holy Spirit as we are being rooted and grounded in love. God's grace in us can accomplish abundantly far more than we can ask or imagine. This is true with the realities of illness, caregiving, and dying.

Whether our enemies are fear, loneliness, loss, unforgiveness, abuse, disappointment, loss of speech, problems with creditors, or radical therapies, we *can* overcome. Enemies seek to swallow us alive, to sweep us away, to rage over us. But because the Lord is on our side, we will be saved. And that is wonderful news!

Paul offered his prayer expressing God's desire or will for us in six ways:

1. that we will have inner strength through the Spirit,
2. that Christ will dwell in our hearts by faith,
3. that we will be rooted and grounded in love,
4. that we will have the power to comprehend the breadth, length, height, and depth of God's love,
5. that we will know and experience the love of Christ, and
6. that we will be filled with the fullness of God.

For Christ and the Holy Spirit to dwell in us means that they abide in us—they make their home in us. Is it any wonder that we get the daily strength to carry on? We need to feel drawn to the fullness of God in our lives; it is a force that draws us confidently forward.

Of the hundreds of patients and family members I have met, there has been only one person I really didn't like. Charlie was a whiner who thought everyone was his enemy. From his perspective, no one was on his side. He was terrified of dying alone, yet he would not let anyone into the process with him. His death was tragic because he did it alone, and he did it poorly. Let it not be so with us! May we be filled with the Spirit and saved from our true enemies.

Prayer Suggestion

Select the part of Paul's prayer that most speaks to your needs. Think about an enemy you face and allow this prayer to become your defense to save you from your enemy. Intentionally read the prayer—say it aloud. Tell that old or new enemy of yours (or of the one you love) to hit the road, for the greatest force in life is your strength.

Prayer

O Lord, if you had not been on our side—we declare together—had you not been on our side, we would have perished beneath the storms of our enemies. We would have been swept away; we would have drowned in the turbulent seas.

But thanks be to God, an Anchor of love and power is holding us. We are being rescued from the raging waters. We are being rooted and grounded in love and grace.

Thanks be to God, for our help is in the Lord who made heaven and earth and all things therein. Amen.

My Soul Is Satisfied

My soul is satisfied as with a rich feast,
and my mouth praises you with joyful lips.
Psalm 63:5

If you had to state today whether or not you are satisfied with your life, what would your answer be? What gives us the ability to be satisfied with our lives? We humans are complex creatures. We have a soul, spirit, heart, and body. Understanding the difference between these parts can be a challenge. In the Hebrew sense, the soul is akin to the totality of a person. The spirit is differentiated as the motive forces in the soul, while the heart is the seat of one's reason, will, and emotions.

Everyone faces difficulties in life. Some people seem to be able to roll with the punches, while others struggle or fail to survive them. Most of us avoid the question of whether or not we are satisfied with our lives because if we answer no, then we face a decision. Either we change our lives to make them more satisfying, or we settle for being dissatisfied. It may seem safer to just not ask the question.

Part of the dying process is an invitation to review and to take stock of our lives. It is to look back over our years, however many they are, and ask ourselves the question, Are we content with our lives or not? Do we find meaning and completeness in the kind of life we have led? While reviewing our lives is a natural part of the dying process, many people never ask the question. Frankly, it is a good spiritual practice to periodically examine ourselves and not wait for illness to trigger it. I know more than one person who would have changed her life if she had asked the question earlier. From my personal experience, a potentially serious illness at thirty-seven years of age caused me to reexamine my life and be open to changes.

Our psalmist has evaluated his life and decided that his soul is well satisfied, as though he has eaten a rich feast. His life has been good. He has faced trials and spent time in the dry and weary land, but his soul has repeatedly found help in God, and he is blessed. Now as he faces new adversities, he clings to God with the faith and assurance that God will uphold him again. Psalm 63 is one of the most beautiful and popular psalms. May it speak to our hearts today.

PSALM 63:1-8

O God, you are my God, I seek you,
  my soul thirsts for you;
my flesh faints for you,
  as in a dry and weary land where there is no water.
So I have looked upon you in the sanctuary,
  beholding your power and glory.
Because your steadfast love is better than life,
  my lips will praise you.
So I will bless you as long as I live;
I will lift up my hands and call on your name.

My soul is satisfied as with a rich feast,
  and my mouth praises you with joyful lips
when I think of you on my bed,
  and meditate on you in the watches of the night;
for you have been my help,
  and in the shadow of your wings I sing for joy.
My soul clings to you;
  your right hand upholds me.

Jackie amazed me the first time I met her. The occasion was a care team meeting for her mother at the nursing home where she lived. Her mother was my patient and was dying of Parkinson's disease. Jackie was candid with me about her mother and about their family life. Jackie was the middle of three daughters. Her father was an abusive alcoholic who left his negative mark on all the family. According to Jackie, she and her sisters and mother not only became alcoholics, but also they all have achieved sobriety for six or more years. It is amazing and wonderful to think that four out of four family members did the healing work to face their fears and demons and achieve sobriety. This was no easy task for any of them.

Jackie's mother had a terrible and frightening marriage to her father. Years later she met a wonderful gentleman who married the whole family. Their life was marvelous for the first twelve years; then Jackie's mom was diagnosed with Parkinson's disease, and the downhill journey began. For the past four years, her mother had lived in a nursing home. Now she was nearing the end of her earthly journey.

The shadow of God's wings was a familiar place for Jackie and her family. They knew well the terror of the night. They had also experienced individually and as a family the dry and weary land where there is little water. During their first long journey across this land, the family found love, fullness, and sobriety after much courage and hard work. Their souls were satisfied as with a rich feast, and their mouths praised the Lord, for God was their help in time of trouble, a sheltering wing in the face of trouble. Through God's power they all turned their lives around and found sanity, good marriages, and meaning.

Now with the escalation of her mom's illness, Jackie and her family were again in the parched and weary land. This time, however, they were better equipped, for they knew that God would provide water for the journey. Jackie had quickly sought the shelter of God's wings, seeking sanctuary in God's healing, steadfast love. But Jackie had one fear—that her mother would die alone. This idea horrified Jackie because she knew that her mother's greatest fear was being alone. Jackie prayed hard to be at her mom's beside when she died. She sought our prayers too, and we all prayed that her mom would not be alone at the time of her departure. As it turned out, her death occurred in less than a week; all of her family was with her. Being at her mom's bedside was a peaceful blessing for Jackie. It was a good death because her mother was physically comfortable and surrounded by her family.

When I review my life, the psalmist's words come to mind. My soul thirsts after God, for I have found sanctuary and strength in the shadow of God's wings. I love God and yearn for God's loving presence. I know the aching thirst that follows a dry spell of God's loving presence. My life has been extraordinarily blessed, and I have found that God's love is better than life itself. I praise God for all my blessings. If I were to die today, at age fifty-two, I could not complain. My soul is well satisfied because life has been a great gift to me.

What surprises me is how many times I've had to remind myself during times of trials to turn to God for help. I know from past experience that God helps me through my problems, so it seems strange that I don't always think first of turning to God. Often I have to get uncomfortable with a problem before I seek God's help. I am the one who forgets to be steadfast. When I realize that I am in a dry and arid place, I recognize that I need God's help and seek it.

I have known many people who died between ages thirty-five and sixty-five whose lives were full and souls were well satisfied. Faith was the key to their seeking sanctuary under God's wings, where they discovered unconditional love, nurture, and strength. Like Jackie and her family, they found that they could make it through the valley of the shadow of death when they walked beneath God's protective and sheltering wings. May you find such fullness in life and in death.

PRAYER SUGGESTION

Have you ever seen a mother hen gather her chicks under her wings? It is a moving sight. In the presence of danger, the mother hen calls her chicks to her and spreads her wings, carefully sheltering the little ones from view. Sometimes it is nice to imagine ourselves in such shelter, a safe place from which we can peer out at life. Imagine a place that could be such a sanctuary for you, somewhere you could feel safe from danger and safe to be yourself. Relax and find this place in your mind's eye. Then seek it as a shelter during rough times, and share your prayers with God from this safe place.

PRAYER

O God, our hearts yearn and faint for you, for we are like
people traveling through a barren and arid land.
Our souls thirst for your presence and the shelter of your
wings. Deep in the shadow of your protective wings we
would seek shelter from the trials of our lives. Here we
would seek your love and nurture for our souls,
for your love is better than life itself.
You do fill us as with a rich feast. Surely our souls will be
satisfied, and we will sing your praises forever and ever.
Amen.

How to Love God

Those who love me, I will deliver;
I will protect those who know my name.

. . . .

With long life I will satisfy them,
and show them my salvation.
Psalm 91:14, 16

In 1988 I had the joy of visiting Israel. While there I renewed my baptismal vows in the chilly Jordan River, traveled back and forth across the Sea of Galilee, and tasted the bitterness of the Dead Sea. These three connected sources of water could not be more different from one other. The Jordan River was cold and beautiful. I saw it when the waters were a pristine green and when the rains had filled it with muddy water. The Jordan River flows into the Sea of Galilee.

The beautiful Sea of Galilee teemed with life. Its smoothness reminded me of mercury. I found the fish markets in Tiberius overflowing with freshly caught fish. In fact, they redefined my concept of fresh fish, as some of the fish were still trying to breathe! The Sea of Galilee flows down into the Dead Sea, which, as its name suggests, contains no life. When our bus pulled up at the Dead Sea, I was amazed to see a man reading a newspaper as he floated on top of the water! The water's density made this possible. The Dead Sea is full of minerals that choke out all life. It is a barren place.

These three water sources could be compared to life. The Dead Sea is like a closed person whose life is an end in itself. If we continue to receive from others but do not pass on our blessings, we will stifle the life in ourselves. If, on the other hand, we balance our lives with receiving and giving, we will teem with life. When we are open to life flowing through us to touch others, our lives abound.

One of the promises of Psalm 91 is that those who love God will receive long life and salvation. To be a true statement, "long life" must include eternity, because we know that some people who love God die young. Further, if we understand that our life with God is an everlasting relationship, it helps us to make sense of the bad things that do happen to perfectly good people. Psalm 91 is a majestic psalm affirming God's protective love for us. Our challenge is to know and love God.

PSALM 91

You who live in the shelter of the Most High,
　　who abide in the shadow of the Almighty,
will say to the LORD, "My refuge and my fortress;
　　my God, in whom I trust."
For he will deliver you from the snare of the fowler
　　and from the deadly pestilence;
he will cover you with his pinions,
　　and under his wings you will find refuge;
his faithfulness is a shield and buckler.
You will not fear the terror of the night,
　　or the arrow that flies by day,
　　or the pestilence that stalks in darkness,
　　or the destruction that wastes at noonday.

A thousand may fall at your side,
　　ten thousand at your right hand,
　　but it will not come near you.
You will only look with your eyes
　　and see the punishment of the wicked.

Because you have made the LORD your refuge,
　　the Most High your dwelling place,

no evil shall befall you,
>   no scourge come near your tent.

For he will command his angels concerning you
>   to guard you in all your ways.
On their hands they will bear you up,
>   so that you will not dash your foot against a stone.
You will tread on the lion and the adder,
>   the young lion and the serpent you will trample under
>   foot.

Those who love me, I will deliver;
I will protect those who know my name.
When they call to me, I will answer them;
>   I will be with them in trouble,
>   I will rescue them and honor them.
With long life I will satisfy them,
>   and show them my salvation.

I had read this psalm a number of times, but it did not have significant meaning for me until my mother died in 1995. My dad requested that we sing the marvelous hymn "On Eagle's Wings," which is based on Psalm 91, at her funeral. A little over three months later, the same hymn was sung at the memorial service after the Oklahoma City bombing. The hymn verses restate God's incredible protection as expressed in the psalm—promises such as: "He will deliver you from the snare of the fowler," "You will not fear the terror of the night, or the arrow that flies by day," "A thousand may fall at your side, . . . but it will not come near you," "No evil shall befall you," and "He will command his angels concerning you to guard you in all your ways."

Interestingly, even though we stood in the presence of death, faced with fear, discouragement, and depression, this psalm brought us peace, hope, and comfort. Its words and message deeply touched our souls. Thank God that the Psalms have such power to stir our faith in times of hardship!

Verses 14 and 16 proclaim that those who love God will be delivered, and those who know God's name will be protected; they will receive long life and salvation. Knowing and loving God are important aspects of our lives that deserve our attention and development.

If you desire to love God, I offer you four suggestions.

1. *Spend time alone with God.* This includes time when you are just sitting still, listening—times when you are aware of yourself, your thoughts, and your environment. Solitude with God can also take the shape and form of prayer, scripture reading, studies, singing, art, or dance. The important thing is that during this time you are learning about God, yourself, and the world. The beginning place for learning is to seek to know yourself as you awaken more to the world around you and within you.

2. *Spend time with God in community.* One can feel a sense of community in a church, temple, or mosque; while doing mission work or a community service project; participating in a study group; or meeting for coffee with like-minded friends. The vital ingredient for community is for God to be the center of the activity. For encouragement and growth, we need places where God and faith can be fully discussed and expressed. Community allows us a place to celebrate God and grow in knowledge and love.

3. *Love God by caring for others.* I am convinced that relationships are the most significant part of our lives. Although we frequently list family or friends as top priorities in our lives, the way we treat these relationships does not always reflect their priority. Consciously live out your beliefs in your daily life with the people around you. When you treat people with respect and kindness, they tend to return the goodwill.

   One of the blessings at Hospice Austin is working with a large and wonderful group of volunteers. Many of these people had someone they loved as a patient with Hospice Austin. They want to give back something of what they received, so a year or more after their loved one's death, they take our volunteer training and join our team as helpers. Regardless of any presence or absence of religious affiliation, each of these people loves God by seeking to care for the needs of another.

4. *Love God by enjoying and appreciating the world that surrounds you.* God is certainly more than creation, but the whole universe reveals God. Nature, the seasons of the year, medicine, medical technologies, art, furniture, buildings, knickknacks, and our homes are all nurturing areas in which to enjoy and appreciate God. Be thankful for the good in the world that surrounds you.

Geneva was a sweet, elderly Christian woman afflicted with brain cancer. I never visited Geneva without sensing God's presence. Beside her bed was an old Methodist hymnbook. As Geneva's disease took a toll on her body, she would greet visitors and then go back to sleep. I often sat beside her and sang songs from the hymnal, all the while aware that other people did the same thing for her. I was one of many voices surrounding her with sung prayer, and I felt part of a community of family and friends.

Geneva's weight got down to sixty-two pounds, and for four or five weeks none of us knew why she was still alive. I began to prayerfully ponder what Geneva might be waiting for. During my next visit I anointed her, spoke words of forgiveness, and encouraged her to be released from the brokenness of her body. Six hours later she died. Whether her death had anything to do with what I did, I do not know. What I do know is that I experienced God's love and I loved God through my relationship with Geneva. This was as true when she was unconscious as it was when she was conscious. Each time I came, I lifted her up with prayers, songs, and psalms. Though Geneva lay in her hospital bed a prisoner to her disease, I know that in her heart she knew the shelter of the Most High. As so often happens, both her faith and mine were strengthened by my acts of faith and love with her.

Loving is the work of each of our lives. May you be blessed by receiving and giving love to others. May you be encouraged by the good in your life and strive to love without fear. May you know salvation and a long life.

Prayer Suggestion

Spend some time reflecting on your life. How much time do you spend alone with God? Do you engage in community activities that connect you with

God? What opportunities do you have to express love for God by how you conduct your relationships with others? In what ways can you appreciate the material world that surrounds you? Decide in your heart this day to cultivate your relationship with God by identifying a way you can grow in your knowledge and love of God.

PRAYER

Merciful God, you are our shelter and our dwelling place.
Help us to seek you in our lives.
Free us to love you better, and guide us on our path.
Surround us with protecting angels, and give us confidence
    in your eternal plans for us, even in the presence of ill-
    ness and death. Amen.

WONDERFUL ARE GOD'S WORKS

For it was you who formed my inward parts;
you knit me together in my mother's womb.
I praise you, for I am fearfully and wonderfully made.

Psalm 139:13-14a

My hospice work in the Austin, Texas, area blesses and enriches me enormously. Where else could I meet and minister to such a diverse group of people? Most of my visits are in the home, so I see people in their natural environment.

Austin is a liberal, cosmopolitan city that attracts diversity. I have been fortunate to serve as chaplain to a wonderfully interesting group of people. I have worked with Christians, atheists, agnostics, Buddhists, Jews, Hindus, and an assortment of other religious preferences. I have assisted wealthy, "important" people, as well as anonymous street people. Caucasians, African-Americans, Native Americans, Germans, Filipinos, Hispanics, and others have been my patients. They come from the United States, Canada, Mexico, the Philippines, Japan, Australia, England, Cuba, and other countries. Some never attended school, while others served in the White House.

This rich experience has led me to three conclusions:

1. *God has created marvelously diverse and interesting people.* Diversity is God's plan. Yet, for all of our differences, we are all vulnerable humans who share the same needs for love and meaning.
2. *In God's sight we are all equal.* We are all made in the image of God, with the divine light in each of us. No one is beyond God's love and concern. Consequently, we have no place for prejudice or judgment in our

lives. Only God is qualified as the final Judge. We need to resist the temptation to put down other people because they are different from us.

3. *Love and relationships are the most important things in life.* Only love and memories accompany us in death. We leave behind our bodies, status, accomplishments, and material possessions. Our priorities need to reflect the importance of good, healthy relationships. How we respond to others, whether a person is a grocery store clerk or our spouse, determines our authenticity as genuine, caring persons. Having designed us as unique creatures, God has a plan of possibilities for our lives. We choose which of those possibilities we follow. How we respond to God and life in large part determines our future.

Psalm 139 is a treasure of a psalm, for it gives us insight into our relationship with God and instills confidence in us. As you read it, please take it personally.

PSALM 139:1-18

O LORD, you have searched me and known me.
You know when I sit down and when I rise up;
    you discern my thoughts from far away.
You search out my path and my lying down,
    and are acquainted with all my ways.
Even before a word is on my tongue,
    O LORD, you know it completely.
You hem me in, behind and before,
    and lay your hand upon me.
Such knowledge is too wonderful for me;
    it is so high that I cannot attain it.

Where can I go from your spirit?
    Or where can I flee from your presence?
If I ascend to heaven, you are there;
    if I make my bed in Sheol, you are there.
If I take the wings of the morning

and settle at the farthest limits of the sea,
even there your hand shall lead me,
and your right hand shall hold me fast.
If I say, "Surely the darkness shall cover me,
and the light around me become night,"
even the darkness is not dark to you;
the night is as bright as the day,
for darkness is as light to you.

For it was you who formed my inward parts;
you knit me together in my mother's womb.
I praise you, for I am fearfully
and wonderfully made.
Wonderful are your works;
that I know very well.
My frame was not hidden from you,
when I was being made in secret,
intricately woven in the depths of the earth.
Your eyes beheld my unformed substance.
In your book were written
all the days that were formed for me,
when none of them as yet existed.
How weighty to me are your thoughts, O God!
How vast is the sum of them!
I try to count them—they are more than the sand;
I come to the end—I am still with you.

Psalm 139 is a magnificent psalm that we all need to take to heart. It contains four truths that can work as encouragements in our lives:

1. *God knows us inside out and loves us anyway.* God is fully aware of our most horrible and most honorable deeds. God knows all our thoughts and motives, and in spite of our shortcomings and sins, God always loves us.

As a child, when I learned about the Great Judgment at the end of time, I had a vision of Judgment Day in my mind. We all stood in line awaiting our individual judgment. As we stepped before God, a giant movie screen would flash our whole life by, with our sins, failures, and imperfections illuminated for all to see. In this vision, I saw the judgment as a time of shame and embarrassment for me.

Now as a mature adult, I envision God's opening our hearts so that we have complete self-awareness and knowledge. We will know ourselves as God knows us. Our judgment involves being confronted with the truth. And I cannot image the loving God I know doing this in a way that would humiliate or shame us. Rather, God will present us with the truth in love.

2. *There is nowhere we can go from God's presence.* If we go to the farthest limits of the earth, God is there. If we find ourselves in the greatest darkness, God is there, for darkness is as light to God. Even in death, God is with us, leading and upholding us. We are never alone, for God is our ever-present companion.

Sometimes I feel cornered or lost. Reminding myself that God is with me can open me to possibilities and attitudes previously frozen by fear or anger. Knowing that God is where I am has also stopped me from doing some deeds I might have done if I had really been alone!

3. *God knitted us together in our mothers' wombs; we are fearfully and wonderfully made.* We are all marvelous creations of God, with the spark of divine life in us. Our lives and personalities are not just happenstance but reflective of God's intentions. When we struggle to make peace with ourselves, it helps to remember that God was there when we were being made. If there is something about ourselves that we dislike and cannot change, how freeing it can be to know that God knows all about this. God was there when we were made, and we are fearfully and wonderfully made. Good can be redeemed from whatever our negative situation is, for God has a plan of possibilities for us to live into.

4. *God knows all of our days before they ever existed.* Without getting into a complicated discussion of God's will, let me make a few comments. While all of us must die, God does not necessarily predestine when and how we die. God's perfect will for all of us is that we live rich, long, full lives. Our deaths

may be caused by an accident or illness about which we can do nothing. They may result from someone's poor judgment, including mistakes made by a medical team.

If we really believe it is God's will for us to have cancer, are we not opposing God's will when we fight to eradicate the disease? To say that God has beheld our unformed substance and written in God's book all of our days before we are even formed is to say that God transcends time and knows all things that were, are, and will be. God may know that we will die from cancer at age sixty, but God does not give us cancer so that we will die at that time. The cancer may be the result of our own sowing, or it may simply be caused by heredity. The psalmist's point is that God cares enough about us to know everything, even the number of days that we will live on this earth. Frequently we can look back prior to a person's death and see God's grace-filled fingerprints wooing the person toward healing and growth.

My hope for all of us is that we will take seriously this marvelous gift of life and be good stewards of all the days we have left. May God's grace and our faith carry us through the valley of the shadow of death into new life.

Prayer Suggestion

Consider the four truths from Psalm 139. What does it mean to you personally to understand that God knows you inside out and still loves you? Does it calm or frighten you to think that God is everywhere you are? Remember that you are fearfully and wonderfully made, and trust that the number of days God has given you is enough.

PRAYER

Give us the confidence to trust in you and your love for us,
especially as we walk through the valley of the shadow
of death.
May hope and love be our companions!
Show us how we are fearfully and wonderfully made,
so that we may treasure our lives and those around us.
Shower us with the grace and love to care for others.
May you be praised now and always. Amen and amen.

Notes

INTRODUCTION

1. A footnote in the New Revised Standard Version Bible translates this phrase as "valley of the shadow of death." Subsequent quotations of this verse use the footnoted translation.

PSALM 22: THE VALUE OF OUR FEELINGS

1. It seems remiss not to mention that the dying process also involves emotions like peace, joy, love, fullness, and laughter.

PSALM 13: HOPE IN THE DARKEST VALLEY

1. By "sleep of death," I am not referring to the experience of numbness that can follow shocking news. That is a natural part of grief.

PSALM 100: GOD STICKS WITH US

1. For those who want to reflect on the nature of God's will, I recommend Leslie Weatherhead's book, *The Will of God*.

PSALM 126: THE LAW OF SOWING AND REAPING

1. See Luke 8:4-15.

PSALM 139: WONDERFUL ARE GOD'S WORKS

1. There may be times when God does give us an illness, like Paul's blindness en route to Damascus. The image I wish to dispel is that of God on a throne dispensing illness to one person, a car wreck to another. Someone could walk into this room and shoot me, yet God did not make the person do it. Free will insists that each person bears responsibility for his or her decisions.

About the Author

The Reverend Dr. Ann Hagmann is a chaplain for Hospice Austin, the largest hospice in Central Texas. She is also the founder of Whispering Hope Ministries, an organization that promotes healing and wholeness for individuals and groups through activities such as speaking engagements, retreats, and individual and group coaching.

Ann holds a bachelor of science degree from University of Arkansas, Fayetteville. After teaching junior and senior high school science for two years, she spent fourteen years in management with AT&T and Southwestern Bell before responding to a call to ministry. She attended Perkins School of Theology at Southern Methodist University in Dallas, where she earned the master of divinity and doctor of ministry degrees.

Before moving to the Austin area, Reverend Dr. Ann, as she is known, pastored United Methodist churches in Oklahoma for ten years. She is an ordained elder in The United Methodist Church and a graduate of The Upper Room's Academy for Spiritual Formation. Ann is the author of another Upper Room book, *Climbing the Sycamore Tree: A Study on Choice and Simplicity.* She loves the outdoors, gardening, travel, and adventure.

If you enjoyed *Abiding Hope,* you might also enjoy this book by Ann Hagmann.

Climbing the Sycamore Tree
A Study on Choice and Simplicity

Do you make everyday economic decisions based on your Christian faith and values, or have you been influenced by our materialistic culture? What you discover about yourself and our culture in this study on economic choices and the spiritual discipline of simplicity may surprise you.

Using the story of Zacchaeus as its inspiration, *Climbing the Sycamore Tree* examines economic decision making in light of what Jesus taught. In this six-week study for small groups or individuals, author Ann Hagmann challenges readers to understand culturally acceptable but less than Christian behaviors, and she offers alternative choices.

Hagmann encourages a simple lifestyle that flows from Christlike stewardship and spiritual growth.

ISBN 0-8358-0946-3 • Paperback • 160 pages

To order, call 1-800-972-0433 or order online at www.upperroom.org/bookstore.

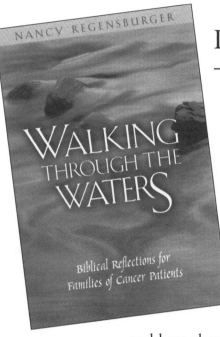